Notes
from Outside the Truman Show

Essays on
MICMAC America

Mark J. Plawecki

Printed in the United States of America.

ISBN: 978-1-59571-976-8
Library of Congress Control Number: 2014904145

Designed and published by

Word Association Publishers
205 Fifth Avenue
Tarentum, Pennsylvania 15084

www.wordassociation.com
1.800.827.7903

To
Hon. MICHAEL SABALA,
FIRST IN LAW
FIRST IN THE JUDICIARY
+ SECOND IN THE HOME RUN
STANDINGS TO WILLIE THE WONDER!
BEST
WISHES,

For Noah and Ryan Pawloski

Born in a century of misguided fear

Contents

The Plan of the Book

This work consists of a compendium of columns written by the author under the pen names Spartacus and (later) Confessions of a Condor, published in the *Detroit Legal News*, from the years 2006-2012. All but one of the columns ("Ike's Warning at Fifty") have been updated during 2013, offering a reassessment of the earlier essays and reflections of the state of our Union as we enter 2014, the centennial of the start of the First World War.

The introduction Q and A conjures up from our heroic yet murky past rivals Theodore Roosevelt, one of the true architects of America's Empire, and Empire opposition leader William Jennings Bryan, one of the most progressive politicians in U.S. history. The former could hardly be pleased that his envisioned empire is now run by giant oligarchic corporations whose ancestors he tried, and had some success in, breaking up. The latter, whose anti-big business stance made him a three-time presidential nominee, was monstrously mythologized in a popular 1950s play (and later film) called *Inherit the Wind*, a happy stroke of good fortune for our present MICMAC masters.

Preface

"Behind the ostensible government sits enthroned an invisible government owing no allegiance and acknowledging no responsibility to the people. To destroy this invisible government, to befoul the unholy alliance between corrupt business and corrupt politics is the first task of the statesmanship of the day."

–Theodore Roosevelt
August 1912

Introduction

William Jennings Bryan and Theodore Roosevelt interview author Mark J. Plawecki, aka Condor.

TR: What is this confounded Truman Show of which you speak?

Con: The Truman Show is a mythological universe inhabited at present by the great majority of Americans. In this universe 1) the United States is a constitutional republic, just like government class textbooks teach, 2) minimal government regulation on business is good for the economy, and 3) the ecological devastation being talked about by environmentalists is either a) someone else's problem or b) admittedly our problem, but one that is manageable (There is also a "c" category-people who deny the devastation altogether. These denialists are presently known as "Republican office holders").

           Belief in two of these three tenets of faith places one deeply entrenched inside The Truman Show. Being a slow learner, Condor did not escape until less than a decade ago. Given the nature, rhythm, and demands of daily life, it is certainly not the fault of most that they exist inside this gigantic bubble.

WJB: How did it get its name?

Con: From two sources. First, there was a 1998 near classic movie *The Truman Show* whose lead character perfectly encapsulates our current collective condition. Second, President Harry Truman (who served from 1945-1953) in early 1947 started us down the road of our long descent away from a republican form of government.

Garry Wills, whose skills "have justly brought him renown as America's greatest public intellectual" (*The Chicago Tribune)*, unsurprisingly penned arguably the finest essay ever written on *any* president in a 1976 *Esquire* piece about Truman (anthologized in 1983's *Lead Time*). Stripping FDR's successor of the mythology with which Condor grew up, Wills traced the beginnings of the Cold War he would later majestically explore in-depth with *Bomb Power* (2010).

I did not read the *Esquire* essay until 1995; even then, I was too inculcated by Truman as American Icon to have it penetrate my dull, propagandized mind. In 1996 I saw Wills deliver an address at Michigan State University. After his talk questions were taken from the audience. He was asked who had been the best and worst presidents since World War II. The best was Eisenhower, Wills replied. "The worst," he added, "was Truman."*

Thus stunned was Condor. That Give 'Em Hell Harry was one of our more able Oval Office occupiers had been etched in stone for me from earliest readings, and David McCullough's then recent (1992) thousand page biography had done nothing to persuade otherwise. It took a long while to understand, through the polluted views U.S. mainstream historians gift us, just how right Wills was. A few years later I read Gore Vidal's succinct, three page dissection of the Truman presidency on why Harry S ("for nothing" wrote Vidal) was his favorite villain; confirmation at its wittiest. Wills and Vidal came from very different backgrounds and viewpoints-particularly about the Christian tradition, on which they were diametrically opposed, but ended up with virtually identical analyses of the 33rd president. This point has not been made before.

TR: What has happened to the Constitution?

Con: Still revered by all-except in name only. Since World War II what Wills calls Bomb Power-the power to decide if and when to use nuclear weapons-has ceded all foreign policy control to the president, making him ostensibly the most powerful person in the world. Yet, paradoxically, these presidents have found themselves, in all other matters, in chains (particularly the second Bush and Obama), totally at the mercy of what I call MICMAC-The Military Industrial Congressional Media Academic Complex.

WJB: How did MICMAC form?

Con: President Dwight Eisenhower's Farewell Address in 1961 contained a warning of the dangers of what he called the "military industrial complex" which had arisen from World War II. MIC turning into MICMAC came into clear focus, for me, after the 2006 mid-term elections. The Democrats had retaken both chambers of Congress, Bush's foreign policy was finally resonating with the public for the disaster that it had always been, and it was clear change was about to come. Except the only change that arrived was an increase in defense spending by the new party in control. Not a peep from mainstream media.

    As a boy in the early 1970s, Condor had played in a Westside Detroit summer baseball league called Mic

Mac. None of us kids knew where the term came from. It turns out Micmac is a First Nations People native to Canada; the Micmac are known as "People of the red earth." ** The league had been founded in nearby Windsor in 1917. That was the year of my father's birth, and also the year Woodrow Wilson took the U.S. into World War I, mere months after being re-elected on the slogan "He kept us out of war."

WJB: I opposed our entry into that conflict-resigning in protest as Wilson's Secretary of State-need I remind you both.

TR: You needn't remind me. I called you at the time "the most contemptible figure we have ever had as Secretary of State." Having seen the last century play out from the netherworld, I soften that pronouncement...a little.

Con: The Mic Mac League emblem was

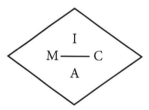

which is perfect because though the Military Industrial Complex controls, it is completely buttressed by MAC (Media, Academia, and Congress). Without near full support from these three institutions, it could not hold total dominion over the population.

A sublime recent example (November 2013) concerns Pentagon bookkeeping. Accounting employees for the Department of Defense simply "plug in" false data to match up with what the Treasury Department expects to see. This investigation, done by the wire service Reuters, went back to 1996 and covered $8.5 trillion of taxpayer funds.

One might think this an important story- but apparently it wasn't important enough for ABC, CBS, CNN, or Fox News to report about. This would be beyond rationality, except that media subservience to the military is standard operating procedure in MICMAC.

TR: What is your view of the Apocalypse? Is it as fundamentalist as our friend Bryan here?

Con: It has already arrived. It just doesn't happen overnight. Rene Girard, who is the Darwin of our times, says it began at Verdun in 1916-the senseless French/German "escalation to extremes" battle that slaughtered 800,000 men, which only sowed the seeds for an even more horrific confrontation that began less than a quarter century later. World War II saw the culmination of Europe's mimetic conflict that began with Napoleon Bonaparte; it remains the greatest tragedy in mankind's history-up to now. Today, however, in the U.S. we glorify this conflict like no other; it's even known to many as "The Good War." We honor and praise the war, rerun endless "feel good" Hollywood movies about it, forget the destruction it caused.

World War II produced the Holocaust-the mass extermination of nearly six million Jews-which is rightly portrayed as the worst event in the annals of our species. Erased from memory, though, is Hitler's speech to his generals on August 22, 1939, where he announced his plan to eliminate the entire Polish race, "men, women, and children," so that the master race could have its needed "living space" *(Lebensraum)* after

Poland was conquered. Two to three million ethnic Poles died as a result-no one outside Poland remembers-and his plan was to kill all except those who were to be made slaves for the Third Reich. He just didn't have enough time.

WJB: But the Western Allies won the war. Democracy prevailed. What's happened since?

Con: In the U.S., democracy has degenerated into what John Nichols and Robert McChesney accurately call "Dollarocracy." Any talk of government by and for the people is pure absurdity. Members of Congress spend a large portion of each working day contacting potential donors, and these donors are never part of the poor, working, middle, or even upper middle classes. The rich alone are needed. The rich alone get rewarded. Money raised and spent in elections has become frightfully obscene even by the nauseating standards from just a decade ago.

The United States has become, plainly and simply, a global empire. The fact that we have well over *one thousand* military bases around the world is never mentioned in polite circles, in MICMAC media, or anywhere inside The Truman Show. Military budgets cannot even be discussed, except at the margins. Thanks to remarkably unreported greater than $5 billion annual advertising to the U.S. public, the military maintains the highest support (76% approval rating in one recent poll) among Americans compared to all other major institutions. Meanwhile, it eats away, like a cancer, ever larger portions of the nation's body and soul.

TR: Who is Edward Snowden?

Con: In 2013, Mr. Snowden, working for a private contractor that was hired by the National Security Agency, released thousands of documents to the British *Guardian* newspaper, in effect blowing the whistle on the illegal and totalitarian-like surveillance state of the U.S. intelligence establishment. He became a U.S. fugitive, and is currently living in Russia, seeking asylum. MICMAC immediately demonized him as an enemy of the U.S., but as a steady stream of revelations only made the surveillance crowd look more like communist East Germany's infamous Stasi, except with many greater tools to use against its citizens, Snowden's actions gained him a majority approval rating with the American public. Whether the government's massive monitoring of everyday Americans will be curtailed is an open question at this time.

WJB: What is this much ballyhooed 1% vs. 99% split I keep hearing about?

Con: Since 1980, the top 1% of individuals in the U.S. has gained an ever burgeoning share of the nation's wealth. Today, that share (40% is owned by the 1%) is the largest it has been since the Gilded Age.

The key split, rarely reported, is actually between the top 1% and bottom 90%. Forgotten is the 9% below the 1%-which is where Condor and many of his friends fit in-judges, most attorneys, middle-to-upper middle corporate management, college professors-who live comfortably by any standard in the world except that of the 1%, who by and large support the 1% by emulating them, and who do nothing as the super rich rip off the rest of the country. Rather than rebel or even speak out, we in this class find it much easier to sit back, relax, worry about our favorite professional, college, or fantasy sports teams, and ignore the world at large. We live the American Dream, as it was advertised to us since our childhoods, while most of our fellow citizens' dreams turn into nightmares. But a successful attorney friend recently mused to me, "There's plenty of stashed liquor for the coming catastrophe."

The other caveat is that it's really the top .01%, or the 1% of the 1%, who exercise effective control of our politics. This infinitesimally small group accounts for about a quarter of political donations to congressional and presidential candidates, and an unfathomable 80% of the money raised by the two main national parties. This translates into government by and for multimillionaires, billionaires, and large corporations. It's becoming an oligarchy.

TR: Where do the multinationals fit into all this? Aren't there any trustbusters left?

Con: Boeing was just awarded (November 12, 2013) the largest tax subsidy in history. The state of Washington said it would eat $8.7 billion over the next 27 years to keep Boeing's proposed commercial airliner jobs in its bailiwick. And that wasn't enough for the company that has received a net balance of $1.8 billion in federal tax refunds over the past decade. Its secret list of demands to 15 prospective states was shortly thereafter leaked; the giant welfare queen demanded additional tax breaks and cost reductions to set up shop in any of these states. Then the company *still* threatened to cut benefits for its employees. The accelerator of inequality between top corporate management and the rest of a company's workers is thus pushed down further yet.

One week after Boeing's coup, the U.S. Justice Department came to terms with J.P. Morgan, the bank most symbolic of the U.S. financial collapse of 2008. No executives from J.P. Morgan or the other five mega-banks which now comprise assets of 64% of U.S. Gross Domestic Product have been prosecuted, let alone convicted, of the crimes committed by their self-enrichment schemes. The government touted the collective civil fine for Morgan of $13 billion as the largest in history, but 1) $13 billion represents about one half of Morgan's yearly profits, and 2) $11 billion of the fine is tax deductible (this tiny fact escaped the *Wall Street Journal's* otherwise comprehensive account of the settlement). So the taxpayers will, in effect, bail out J.P. Morgan and its financially lecherous top management yet again.

WJB: What about unions? They were practically non-existent when the Rough Rider and I roamed the nation stumping for votes.

Con: Unions, which grew in the 1930s and 1940s, and peaked as a percentage of the total U.S. workforce in 1954 (at 35%), enjoyed a great run until about 1980. In a very real sense, unions built the American middle class. Private sector unions have been completely decimated in the last three-and-one-half decades-declining from 36% of the total private sector jobs in 1953 to 24% in 1979 to 7% today. This was purposely done to scale back all gains working people had achieved, destroy any increasing equality of wealth, and allow corporate profits to flow unimpeded back to the top, as they did before unions existed. The American public largely cheered on this destruction with smug satisfaction, until it belatedly realized what had happened.

A holiday party Condor attended after Reagan's re-election in 1984 is recalled. I was one of two individuals out of about two dozen present from my suburban Detroit high school who'd voted for Mondale; the chief reason given by the others for their support of Reagan was to stop "lazy unions" from gaining too much power. This was at a time when unions were already in decline, and these were the middle class children and grandchildren of the generations which had struggled mightily so that we could enjoy the fruits of their hard fought victories. Virtually all of us had recently graduated from four year universities in Michigan, the birthplace of the United Auto Workers, but nothing we learned in those institutions taught us to value what had been achieved for our behalf. The name Walter Reuther elicited a roomful of blank stares.

Today, the last bastion of union strength lies in the public sector (36% of these jobs are unionized), but here there is general sentiment against unions because of how some local government officials have given away disproportionate retirement packages to certain employees that are straining future municipal and state budgets. Overall, unions are back to representing less than 12% of the U.S. workforce, about the same ratio as they had in 1916. It's taken almost a century, but the robber barons, with ample MICMAC support, have neatly pulled off a reclaiming of complete power. Symbolizing this coup, Michigan in 2013 became a right-to-work state.

TR: How serious is climate change?

Con: In terms Americans of your time may not have understood, but those of today do, this hypothetical may be useful:

You're 48 years old and not feeling well. You go see a doctor. An x-ray shows a spot on your lung. You're not sure what to do.

Fortunately, the top 100 lung specialists in the world are available to review your x-ray and medical records. One says, "It's not cancer. You have nothing to seriously worry about." Two doctors conclude, "It is cancer. But there is little evidence that it has been caused by smoking. You may, if you wish, continue to smoke."

The other 97 doctors determine as follows, "It is cancer and your two-pack-a-day cigarette smoking habit for the past 32 years has caused it. You need surgery ASAP, and, naturally, *QUIT SMOKING NOW*!

What would you do?

This is approximately the predicament the human species finds itself at the end of 2013. Ninety-seven percent of climate scientists, that is, people educated in climate science who actually study climate for a living, say global warming is happening and man is causing it, predominantly by the burning of fossil fuels.

But the world's leaders say, "Well, maybe the 1% of scientists is right (we listen to the 1% in every other area). Or perhaps the 97% are mostly correct-but there is still some time to smoke (we'll cut back to a pack-and-a-half per day) before we get bad enough to really need surgery. We've got a debt crisis, or a war to start, or unemployment to deal with before our next election. We'll deal with climate change...later."

Later is now. There is no longer anything humans can do to stop the early effects of climate change-the evidence mounts daily that it is already here. What we *can* do is mitigate the damage. In law this doctrine imposes on an injured party "the duty to exercise reasonable diligence and ordinary care in attempting to minimize his damages after injury has been inflicted." Unfortunately, man is both injuring and injured party, and law has failed and will continue to fail to stem the gathering and looming tide.

WJB: Getting back to the Apocalypse...the Christian Revelation will be proven right after all, yes?

Con: I think so...just not in the way the fundamentalists would have us believe. The Apocalypse means literally "unveiling" or "uncovering" and doesn't *necessarily* portend the end of the world. But there are troubling developments which up to now have been politically off limits. MICMAC cynically supports a noticeably fragile Israeli democracy which contains increasingly self-destructive elements; MICMAC does so because it profits handsomely from the annual multi-billion dollar U.S. taxpayer subsidy to the tiny Middle East nation of 7.9 million people, much of which is recycled back into MICMAC coffers. The powerful behind-the-scenes Israeli lobby American Israel Public Affairs Committee (AIPAC) plays a pivotal role here, rabidly supported by an American Religious Right Rapturously removed from reality but anxiously awaiting Armageddon.

Whether Max Blumenthal's courageously frank *Goliath* can become a nonfictional *Uncle Tom's Cabin*, in terms of opening the eyes of U.S. men and women of goodwill, plus rallying pure pragmatists who wish to see America rebound from the low esteem it is currently held in throughout most of the world, is very much doubtful. Whether another U.S. President could politically withstand giving an order to an Israeli prime minister to "stop the bombing" as Reagan did in 1982 regarding Menachem Begin's assault of Lebanon is also questionable, though the recent P5+1 interim deal with Iran sheds a ray of hope.***

Girard's *Battling to the End*, released in late 2009, is instructive. Believing that Christian fundamentalists have a mythological conception of the Almighty, he writes, "They think that the violence at the end of time will come from God himself. They cannot do without a cruel God. Strangely, they do not see that violence we ourselves are in the process of amassing and that is looming over our own heads is entirely sufficient to trigger the worst. They have no sense of humor."

We can apply Girard's insight equally to Jewish and Muslim fanatics as well. For sizeable strains in all three major monotheistic religions, a cruel God is a just God. But they each ignore a secret Girard has unlocked for all, which will be addressed in the final columns of this exercise.

---

*   Remember, this was before Bush II and Obama.

**   Given global warming, MICMAC will turn out a doubly appropriate moniker.

*** As this book went to press, 59 U.S. Senators proudly indicated their support for AIPAC by sponsoring new sanctions on Iran legislation that would effectively scuttle the P5+1 deal. Obama has threatened to veto the legislation; AIPAC needed eight more votes to override his veto.

Chapter One

Wrestling with Reality

"...a continuation of the present policy will eventually destroy America. We are already $8 trillion in debt. Most of the world views us as a rogue nation. Our manufacturing base is being depleted, not to mention our natural resources. Our education system is sick. Our culture is decadent. Our government is corrupt."

—**Charley Reese**,
March 18, 2006

On the upside, most American workers completed their brackets in time for the start of the NCAA basketball tournament.

The vast military-industrial complex warning that Dwight Eisenhower so presciently gave in his Farewell Address has an added pillar, and is given new urgency today. The latest credible cost estimates of the Iraq debacle have grown, if trends continue, beyond $1 trillion. This figure is, as my freshman math teacher Father French would say, "a little bit more" than the under $50 billion price tag Defense Secretary Donald Rumsfeld announced three years ago. But Mr. "Stuff Happens" evidently had reason to be mistaken.

Promoting the Bush administration's practice of torture, habeas corpus violations, and illegal spying with open declarations that the commander-in-chief is above U.S. law may produce silence on the right, but there are those getting nervous. Rumsfeld, more that any other single figure, should be held accountable for his policy of, in the words of America's greatest intellect, "destroying the military," and also the carrying to extreme our masochistic support of ally Israel's own military machine.

A new 12,800 word study produced by Harvard University and the University of Chicago academically documents what very few Americans know, or are allowed to know: *uncritical* (as opposed to

1

qualified) support of Israel hurts U.S. interests. This support, ironically, also hurts Israeli interests, since that nation's innocent citizens ultimately suffer the consequences of Arab-extremist retaliation for said policies.

The war hawk neocon cabal in the Defense Department, let by Mr. Rumsfeld, has unilaterally set aside American concerns for years now. And Mr. Rumsfeld is the one person in the U.S. government who *should have known better.*

We certainly could not have relied upon George W. Bush, whose foreign policy experience upon taking office in 2001 consisted of an interest in how much liquor was produced in the Caribbean.

We could not, in retrospect, have relied upon Dick "Birdman" Cheney, who had "other priorities" during his learning curve years (i.e. the Vietnam Era), and would end up restating Charles Wilson's General Motors mantra as "What's good for Halliburton is good for the U.S.A."

We could not, though many had hopes, have relied upon the decent but ultimately timid gentleman-soldier Colin "Mobile Labs" Powell, who must now spend his remaining career living down his farcical 2003 performance at the United Nations.

"Turning our backs on postwar Iraq today would be the modern equivalent of handing postwar Germany back to the Nazis," now sayeth Mr. Rumsfeld.

Think, for a moment, of the enormous erroneousness of such a statement. That this individual *still* holds a position of power speaks volumes of the vast wasteland that is the present American political structure.

It was Rumsfeld, former three-term-plus liberal GOP congressman (when there was such an animal) from suburban Chicago, and *former Secretary of Defense*, who was perfectly placed to be the Voice of Reason after 9/11. But the amateur wrestling star apparently suffered a delayed reaction to a violent reverse takedown, and it's been Keystone Kops' incoherence since ("as we know, there are known knowns; there are also things we know we know, we also know there are known unknowns; that is to say we know there are some things we do not know. But there are also unknown unknowns–the ones we don't know we don't know").

The striking comparisons between Vietnam and Iraq (as opposed to Iraq and Nazi Germany) have been well noted elsewhere. The greatest, of course is the LBJ/GWB administrations' need to keep the American people from knowing what was (is) going on. In this respect, today's mainstream media has been completely compliant. But to hearken back to the great chronicler of the former disaster, one finds no comfort in the truth of David Halberstam's late-in-the-day words: "And so the war went on, tearing at this country; a sense of numbness seemed to replace an earlier anger. There was, Americans were finding, no light at the end of the tunnel, only greater darkness."

–March 2006

Reality Revealed

Two years after "Wrestling with Reality" was printed, Nobel Prize winner in Economics Joseph Stiglitz released a more comprehensive study of Iraq War costs. It said that $3 trillion would be the minimum amount owed by U.S. taxpayers (Rumsfeld's "under $50 billion" estimate had been accompanied with a retort of "Baloney" by the Defense Secretary when a TV interviewer repeated a suggestion that it might be as high as $300 billion). Factoring in weapons, operations, future health care needs for young veterans, interest on foreign loans to fund the war, and future borrowing, the total sum could surpass $5 trillion. Original estimates would thus be off by a factor of one hundred.

Stiglitz's figures did not take into account the hundreds of thousands of Iraqis killed during the conflict, the 2-4 million more displaced from their homes, or the destruction of large amounts of Iraq's infrastructure. They did not include growing numbers of miscarriages, deaths, birth defects, and congenital illnesses among babies in Fallujah, where the U.S. in 2004, targeting insurgents, had bombed white phosphorus and other toxins with impunity. Ten reported bombing incidents in the first eight months of 2012 alone tallied 682 minimum deaths, belying the narrative the U.S. invasion has made Iraq better off. And despite the Obama Administration's spin to the contrary. U.S. forces only left Iraq because the Iraqi government wouldn't grant criminal immunity to our troops under a negotiated Status of Forces Agreement (SOFA).

Rumsfeld's policy of "destroying the military," (as Garry Wills had blunted put it in November 2004), largely succeeded. Stiglitz calls free-market economists "free market fundamentalists," and the guru of this school of thought was the University of Chicago's Milton Friedman. Rumsfeld, as a young Illinois congressman in the early 1960's, latched onto Uncle Miltie's economic theory of complete governmental de-regulation – a fantasy-turned-reality from 1980 to 2008 that ended in the near total collapse of the U.S. financial system, saved only by its huge taxpayer rescue courtesy the U.S. government itself

Friedman's ideas led Rumsfeld to privatize, to the extent possible, the U.S. military. Due to plain greed, Rummy began earning enormous profits from MICMAC, profits nicely documented by Naomi Klein's *The Shock Doctrine* (2007). During his term as Defense Secretary (2001-06), when public officials are suppose to blind trust their assets, Rumsfeld's Gilead stocks increased 807%, thanks largely to the Pentagon's $58 million purchase in 2005 of Gilead-made Tamiflu. Other defense and disaster-related companies Rumsfeld held stock in also saw their fortunes rise during his tenure, and Klein plainly termed the former Princeton wrestling captain, with Dick Cheney and other War on Terror architects, a breed "for whom wars and other disasters are indeed ends in themselves."

Due to plain greed, Rummy began earning enormous profits from MICMAC...

Friedman wrote in 1998 that Ronald Reagan's biggest mistake, including those of his presidency, was not naming Rumsfeld his 1980 running mate. Then the "sorry Bush-Clinton period would never have happened." MF did not live long enough to see his protégé resign in disgrace in November 2006, with GOP leaders upset that his resignation hadn't become known *before* the election, (which might have allowed them, they said, to keep Senate control).

Three months after the Harvard-Chicago study conducted by Professors John Mearsheimer and Stephen Walt (referred to in the previous essay), Michael Massing wrote an exhaustive review of it in *The New York Review of Books*. In a balanced piece where he pointed out numerous errors the authors had made, Massing wrote, "On their central point – the power of the Israeli lobby and the negative effect it has had on U.S. policy – Mearsheimer and Walt are entirely correct."

It is difficult to overestimate the significance of Massing's analysis, yet most Americans are still not only unaware of the immense clout of the Israeli lobby, they are actually unaware of the Lobby's mere existence. The sun in the Lobby's solar system is the American Israel Public Affairs Committee (AIPAC), which has not had an investigative report conducted on its activities on American television since 1977. This despite it being consistently ranked among the most powerful interest groups in Washington (along with the NRA and AARP).

Declassified documents released in 2008 provide substantial evidence that AIPAC, as former Arkansas Senator William Fulbright argued in the 1970s, should be registered as a foreign lobby. The elaborate deception concocted by its founder, Israeli government official Isaiah Kenen, to turn AIPAC into an "American" lobby represents a coup unprecedented in modern public relations annals.

–January 2013

Chapter Two

America's Holocaust

At a recent C-Span broadcast forum on U.S.-Iranian history, an Italian journalist asked about the meaning of the Zogby International poll showing 53% of Americans favoring an attack on the erstwhile Persia. Panelist Stephen Kinzer, former *New York Times* Istanbul bureau chief, exasperatingly responded that the press had been shamefully fanning the flames of war as it did with Iraq, but "I have to say we share this distinction with most of the principal institutions of the United States. The Supreme Court has become a wholly-owned subsidiary of the White House, the Congress has effectively liquidated itself as an independent branch of government, the Democratic Party is completely brain dead, so why should the press be any different?"

One thing the principal institutions have been complicit in is what I call the defactobliteration of the U.S. Constitution. Critics will correctly point out the many beatings this quaint document (kudos to Alberto "Gonzo" Gonzales) has previously taken from Lincoln's suspension of habeas corpus to Truman's "police action" in Korea to Reagan's Iran-Contra fumblings. But the assault on Mr. Madison's child has been breathtakingly blitzkriegian in the six years since 9/11.

Naomi Wolf's "Fascist America, in 10 Easy Steps" addresses how General Musharrif's second coup in Pakistan could not only happen here, but that each of the steps "has already been initiated today in the U.S. by the Bush Administration." Items like creating a gulag, or prison system outside the rule of law (Guantanamo Bay), developing a thug caste (Blackwater), setting up illegal international surveillance (the Bushies' insistence that only *overseas* calls by U.S. citizens were being intercepted turns out to have been a canard) and harassing citizens' groups (government infiltration of dozens of anti-war meetings/rallies under the guise of "suspicious incidents" in the never-meant-to-be-ending War on Terror) are just a few to be noted.

My personal favorite is what Wolf calls "arbitrary detention and release"-the placing of tens of thousands on a list to be security searched if they attempt to fly. Professor Walter F. Murphy, constitutional scholar of no little note at Mr. Madison's own College of New Jersey (Princeton for you modernists), was placed on this terror watch list and denied a boarding pass at Newark this March not, apparently, for his decorated combat marine duty in the aforementioned Korean conflict, but rather for giving a lecture in 2006 critical of Bush's numerous constitutional violations. Unfortunately for this terror suspect, one of the Bush SS was at that moment monitoring C-Span, the channel broadcasting what was once known as free speech, and made the appropriate designation.

The Greek term *Holokauston* is defined as "a completely burnt sacrificial offering to a god." Bush's god is a strange entity who has lead his servant to undertake strange tasks, like expend the lives of more than 4000 citizens in a foreign land for a premise now long established to have been baseless, not to mention fraudulent. Yet his same crew of neocon henchmen, spiritual disciples of Trotsky and Strauss that they are, continually drumbeat for an Iranian sequel to the Iraq madness, and the Pentagon Junta, which ultimately controls such decisions, bides its time while counting its taxpayer-gifted largess.

In order to have faithfully served its god, this Presidential Pontificate not only decided to abuse but, in reality, put to the torch our nation's most revered and sacred document. This is the meaning of the Bush Holocaust. Unless the next president is committed and strong enough, like Superman, to somehow reverse the process, its flames may engulf us all.

—November 2006

The Flames Draw Near

Defactobliteration, the term, has admittedly yet to catch on. No mention of it in early 2013 when Googled. But Much Ado about Very Little; many Shakespearean words and phrases also took awhile to be popularized.

Defactobliteration, the reality, with regard to the U.S. Constitution, is an entirely different matter. Its popularity during the Bush/Cheney Administration proved so irresistible that the successor Obamaites have followed suit as if needing to trump their pathological predecessors. Some seasoned observers believe they have.

"The rule of law," wrote Ralph Nader in 2012, "is rapidly breaking down at the top levels of government." His lament closely followed a *New York Times* expose (May 29, 2012) of the instantly infamous secret "Kill List" that the Obama White House has initiated. Biographical pictures of those on the list are charmingly known, according to one official, as "baseball cards." President Obama often personally decides which militants (including, most ominously perhaps, U.S. citizens) will be executed, usually via drone, in Pakistan, Afghanistan, Yemen, and other majority Muslim countries. As prosecutor, judge, jury, and executioner, the collective role Nader's junior fellow Harvard Law School graduate has assigned himself bears no relation to anything in the 225 year history of the Constitution.

It has, however, allowed him to avoid charges of being "soft on terrorism" by his political opponents – and in time for the Presidential Election of 2012. Obama's former and current staffers leaked this story for just that purpose, and the President was in fact handily reelected.

Four months after the "Kill List" revelations, a joint NYU/ Stanford Law Schools' report documenting Death by Drone in Pakistan produced three clear and sobering findings 1) civilians are killed at a much higher rate than acknowledged by U.S. officials 2) the existence of drones incessantly hovering overhead in the sky has an emotionally and psychologically terrorizing effect on citizens below, and 3) U.S. drone policy is both "damaging and counterproductive" to U.S. relations with Pakistan, whose inhabitants now view our country in an overwhelmingly negative light.

Warrantless wiretapping, an obvious (before 9/11) violation of the Fourth Amendment was, as noted in the previous column, a favorite illegal activity of Bush & Cheney Inc. But President Obama, despite the pledge of candidate Obama to reign in the abuse, has greatly expanded governmental power in this area (one White House official admitted, "It's like *Invasion of the Body Snatchers*"). Freedom of Information requests by the ACLU showed the Justice Department surveillance devices on U.S. individuals' email and network data increased 361% between 2009 and 2011. More people were surveilled without warrants in Obama's first two years than had been in the *entire previous decade*.

Candidate Obama also pledged to close Guantanamo Bay, the Bush/Cheney gulag which once held 779 foreign detainees, nearly all without charge. Feeble attempts to do so were met with Congressional resistance, so it remains an open black mark on America's image throughout the civilized world. Almost 600 of the so called "worst of the worst" have been released, without virtually any U.S. media attention. Three convictions have been obtained (one of which has been overturned on appeal). One hundred sixty-seven prisoners remain, presumably until the Detroit Lions win another NFL championship.

A note on neoconservatism (and its henchmen), which combines strong support for unregulated economic markets with advocating the use of U.S. military force wherever and whenever possible. Leo Strauss was a German-born political philosopher who taught at the University of Chicago from 1949-1969. The Straussian influence of using deception to achieve state interests was most obvious in the Bush/Cheney colossal lie about Iraq's supposed weapons of mass destruction, which sold the American public on the Iraq War.

Despite it being the most thoroughly discredited ideology in post-slavery America, neoconservatism has yet to wither away and die. Its intellectual leaders, like William Kristol of the *Weekly Standard* and John Podhoretz of *Commentary*, occupy an inordinately prominent place in the media portion of MICMAC. Paradoxically named "think tanks" proliferate, with members continuing to call for an attack on Iran, and otherwise lying in wait to invest in the next vapid GOP candidate (they were quite influential in the ill-fated Mitt Romney campaign). Claes Ryn has persuasively argued that the neocons are not conservative at all, but attempt to hijack an existing order similar to what the Jacobins did to France in the 1790s. To the extent they are thwarted is possibly the extent to which U.S. democracy survives.

> **...neoconservatism has yet to wither away and die.**

−January 2013

Chapter Three

Tipping Points

The sad truth is that, as tragic as the blundering Bush Administration's Iraq venture has been since the idea's concoction in the neocons' minds, it will historically pale next to the monumental neglect given to global warming (or "climate change," the term GOP pollster Frank Luntz advised GWB to use because it was less "emotionally challenging" for voters.) Though too few of our fellow citizens know it, we are now dangerously near the "tipping point"-which scientists have warned us about for a decade-the point at which cataclysmic weather-related consequences will be impossible to avoid.

Long forgotten is GWB's campaign pledge of September, 2000, to seek a bill that would cut coal-burning power plants' emission of carbon dioxide (which produce 40% of U.S. carbon dioxide output), the largest agent of global warming. In March, 2001, Bush-appointed EPA director Christine Todd Whitman announced the Administration's support of just such legislation. But the right wing base of the GOP went apoplectic.

"This is a colossal mistake," intoned Myron Ebell, director of global warming policy at the Competitive Enterprise Institute. "If they persist, there will be war."

Thanks to Dick Cheney, Spencer Abraham, and an energy lobby that had contributed $10 million to Republicans in the previous campaign cycle, this war was avoided, and one on the rest of the planet begun. In a stunning reversal three days later, the Bushies released a statement that any regulation of carbon emissions would lead to "significantly higher energy prices" and the effort was ended.

With Bush and Earth, the adage "Nero fiddled while Rome burned" has taken on exponential meaning. In early 2001, the Intergovernmental Panel on Climate Change, composed of nearly every leading climatologist in the world, released its third five-year assessment, leaving little doubt of man's role in global warming. The National Academy of Sciences, *at Bush's request*, then confirmed the results. The Kyoto accords, negotiated during the Clinton years and adhered to by every nation but the U.S. (after Bush opposed it) and Australia, removed the change that even modest emissions reduction would occur. The years 2006, 2005, 1998, 2002, 2004, and 2003 have been the warmest since record keeping began in 1880, and 2007 has already seen the hottest January ever.

Worse yet, the 382 carbon parts per million (ppm) in the atmosphere continues to rise-it was 275 ppm before the industrial revolution. The leading expert on the subject, Dr. James Hansen of NASA (whose testimony before Congress in 1988 can arguably be noted as the start of the Global Warming Era), says there is little time left-a decade at most-in which major change must begin, or we'll reach 450 ppm, the point at which the planet surpasses a temperature in the range it has had for the past million years. *Sea level will rise eighty feet.*

Sea level will rise eighty feet.

Why no general alarm? It's hard to blame the public. The corporate media has been unflinchingly agreeable to providing equal time to energy-funded charlatans who offer no credible evidence to counter the actual scientific data. So people who don't read science journals (most of us) but rely on newsprint and television to be informed are understandably left confused. And political leadership, in both major parties, has been virtually non-existent.

But things might be changing. Five western governors, fed up with federal inaction, recently signed a pact to reduce greenhouse gases 25% by 2025. Eight-six of the country's leading evangelical scholars and pastors have signed the Evangelical Climate Initiative, which calls for federal laws to reduce carbon dioxide emissions, signaling that a powerful political bloc is potentially moving in a positive direction. And when Al Gore testifies this month before John Dingell's House Committee on Energy and Commerce, a slumbering American segment may be awakened. After all, there should enough drama for even the reality-TV-obsessed crowd.

–March 2007

Zeus's Revenge

Six Years after "Tipping Points" the results can be sadly and catatonically conveyed: 1) The effects of global warming have begun to manifest themselves in increasingly spectacular ways 2) The scientific evidence is overwhelming that even more dire consequences than previously predicted are in store for us, the most ominous in the recorded history of man, and 3) Not enough people north of the Rio Grande give a damn to make a dime's worth difference.

The Pew Research Center conducts an annual survey that lists issues Americans consider their government should give "top priority" to. Since 2009, the percentage of respondents who consider global warming important has been 30 (2009), 28 (2010), 26 (2011), 25 (2012), and 28 (2013), each time dead last on a list of 20 issues (strengthening the economy was first in 2013, at 86%). Apparently, it's going to take about four more Hurricane Sandys to awaken the U.S. public.

Global warming offers classic proof of Condor's Truman Show hypothesis. Of 195 United Nations countries, 191 have ratified the Kyoto Protocol of 1997 (implemented in 2005) to stabilize greenhouse gas emissions and prevent catastrophic anthropogenic climate change. The four that have not include tax -haven Andorra (pop.85,000), and three cornerstone representatives of enlightened modern civilization: Afghanistan, South Sudan, and the United States of America. A fifth country, Canada, ratified Kyoto, but pulled out in 2011 when it realized it will be more profitable in the short run to keep emitting its enormous energy reserves (third largest in the world); an unlivable planet for many species, including perhaps its own, will be future generations' concerns.

Clive Hamilton's *Requiem for a Species* gives insight to why the human race has failed to slow down, let alone derail, the oncoming worldwide freight train. First, all governments are obsessed with economic growth, the standard by which all measure themselves. Second, the *individual* is obsessed with consuming more and more material goods, the main standard by which we individually measure ourselves. Third, man has become almost completed disconnected from nature (as long as the A/C and furnace work, extreme weather seems a manageable annoyance).

man has become almost completed disconnected from nature

Cognitive dissonance, which describes what people often feel when confronted with facts that contradict deeply held beliefs, is a fourth reason Hamilton cites. This theory's founder, Leon Festinger, learned that when firm views are "repudiated by the emergence of facts, (people) often begin to proselytize even more fervently after the facts become incontrovertible." This explains why in 1997 48% of self-identifying U.S. Republicans believed the effects of global warming had begun, but after a decade of mountainous confirming evidence, the number had dropped to 24% (Democrat "believers" went from 52% to 76% over the same span).

Hamilton also mentions Prometheus who, in both Greek mythology and tragedy, introduced fire and all gifts of enlightenment (agriculture, medicine, architecture, etc) to man. For these acts, because done in defiance of the ruler of gods and men, Zeus chained him to a rock for untold many years, and also had an eagle daily devour a regenerative liver that nightly grew back.

But while mythology always distorts truth, in this case the tragedy *Prometheus Bound* by Aeschylus (the earliest of the 5th century BCE Greek tragic poets) affirms it. Hamilton focuses on the gifts of enlightenment, which were in the 18th century were interpreted as unleashing the powers of technology and industry. But Hamilton fails to mention perhaps the most important event of all.

In Aeschylus's play, when the chorus asks Prometheus what he did *first* for mankind, the exchange is as follows:

> **Prometheus:** I stopped mortals from foreseeing doom.
> **Chorus:** What cure did you discover for the sickness?
> **Prometheus:** I sowed in them blind hopes.
> **Chorus:** That was a great help that you gave to men.

It is not only the deniers, as hysterical as they are. There is something in the nature of man, which Aeschylus understands, that rejects doom on an individual level. This keeps man, who has no foreknowledge of his day of death, from giving up even against the tallest of odds. Primitive man, like the animal he evolved from, *did* have a sense of his doom.* But Prometheus, in this tradition, gives man "blind hopes" in his struggle against nature. This device is a large reason man has progressed from caves to high-rise condominiums.

Unfortunately, the flipside has now been shown. Since thousands of years of optimism are being thwarted by a seemingly impossible phenomenon – man changes climate – and because to deal with it imperils the vision of our self-believing story of never-ending progress – we're incapable of doing so. And so we will not, until it is too late. This is the tragedy Hamilton convincingly demonstrates that awaits us. "More than ever," proclaims our modern Darwin, Rene Girard, "I am convinced that history has meaning, and that its meaning is terrifying."

---

* David Grene's introduction to his translation of *Prometheus Bound* provided the inspiration for this thought.

–February 2013

Chapter Four

Lurching Columnists and the Children of God

The American film classic *Butch Cassidy and the Sundance Kid* contains a scene in which the two outlaws, having been freelancing without their Hole-in-the-Wall compatriots, return to the gang, only to find an attempted coup being executed. The takeover is led by deep-voiced brute Harvey Logan (played by Ted Cassidy of *Addams Family* Lurch fame). Paul Newman's Butch asks incredulously, "You guys can't want *Logan*!" then proceeds to memorably dispatch the threat ("Rules? In a knife fight? No rules!") with one well-placed swift kick.

Another unfortunate Logan was Dr. George of that name who, in 1798, went to France on behalf of his friend Thomas Jefferson. Sadly for Doc Logan, Mr. Jefferson, then Vice-President, was not getting along with either President John Adams or the Federalist majority in Congress. The Feds proceeded to pass a law prohibiting U.S. citizens from carrying on "correspondence or intercourse" with foreign governments "in relation to disputes or controversies of the U.S."

This partisan act, brought in the same year by the same bunch who gave us the historically repudiated Sedition Act (which made it a crime to publish *anything critical* of the President or Congress-but not the VP-sorry, Mr. Jefferson) has not seen a prosecution in its more than 200 year tenure. The hysterical portion of today's Right wishes to revive Logan for, of all things, Speaker Nancy Pelosi's visit to Syria.

The *Wall Street Journal* has shamefully printed a column by a lawyer named Robert F. Turner, who hallucinogenically stated Pelosi "may well have committed a felony" in going to Syria. Since the folk he admires in Washington have no clue how to conduct foreign policy, it is unsurprising Mr. Turner would take such a position.

What may raise eyebrows is why Michigan Court of Appeals Judge William Whitbeck would, in this publication, embarrass himself by toting the party line on this issue. After bizarrely criticizing former President Jimmy Carter (apparently decades-long tireless work on behalf of Habitat for Humanity makes Carter a "self-obsessed fool"), the good Judge calls the Speaker's trip "a clear violation of the Logan Act."

The Congressional Research Service released a report to Congress last year entitled "Conducting Foreign Policy without Authority: The Logan Act," which provides an updated summary of the law in fourteen footnoted pages. The first sentence of the Introduction states, "The Logan Act is designed to cover relations between private citizens of the U.S. and foreign governments." Earth to Whitbeck-Pelosi is second in line to the Presidency, and as such is not quite a private citizen.

Moreover, her visit was made through normal diplomatic channels; by its own acknowledgment, the State Department briefed the Speaker before she ventured to the Middle East.

The Iraq Study Group, mandated by the U.S. government and co-led by James Baker (if memory serves, the same guy who conducted the first President Bush's foreign policy), urged reopening talks with Syria–a country that, much to the neocons' chagrin, we're not currently at war with.

Finally, four other Congressmen, all Republicans, also visited with high Syrian officials at approximately the

Finally, four other Congressmen, all Republicans, also visited with high Syrian officials...

same time as poor Nancy. Perhaps, though, like the old Federalist law, it should be a crime only when *Democrats* take the road to Damascus.

For the horrible sin of attempting to get two countries with enormous distrust of each other (Syria and Israel) to "resume the peace process," Pelosi is peppered with prevaricating purblindness by the provocative War Machine. Matthew's reported "Blessed are the peacemakers" plea gets pushed aside again.

–November 2007

American "Commies"

The "provocative War Machine" has been cranked up to produce an ever increasing number of interventions since "Lurching Columnists" was written in late 2007. As economist Joseph Schumpeteer noted of the Roman Empire, "There was no corner of the known world where some interest was not alleged to be in danger or under actual attack. If the interests were not Roman, they were those of Rome's allies; and if Rome had no allies, the allies would be invented." Simply omit "known" from the above quote and one has fairly approximated the condition of early 21st century America.

The Pentagon has divided the world into six little publicized regions of "Command," with a seventh-Strategic Command (STRATCOM) handling nuclear weapons, space and cyberspace. * AFRICOM, the latest to be added, was established in 2007 to cover all 54 African countries except Egypt (which is in CENTCOM). African follows PACCOM and EUCOM (both initiated in 1947), SOUTHCOM (1963), CENTCOM (1983), and NORTHCOM (2002).

Communism, in its Soviet-style flowering, was a perfect example of a plan to, in Claes Ryn's words, "improve the human condition that placed unlimited power in the hands of a small elite." Militaristic and bureaucratic, the Soviet Union's 1991 sudden retreat from existence enabled the U.S. to claim lone world superpower status. Within a decade, the Department of Defense proclaimed a policy objective of "full spectrum dominance," by 2020, of land, sea, air, space, and information.

Accordingly, the American command structure's current commanders, blessed as they are with over 1000 foreign military bases in 130 countries, virtually unlimited funding by Congress, and a Washington power elite mindset of constant interventionism, can be ironically considered worthy heirs to the defeated Soviet "commies." Our commies (remembering always that ours are the good guys) have the intellectual energy support provided by the likes of William Bennett, William Kristol, and Robert Kagan – all influential voices calling for war on the "entire Islamic terror network" in the fateful days following 9/11. Like fallen General David Petreaus, they represent "the opportunism of people who care more deeply about having the approval of the powers-that-be and about advancement in their careers than about their own deepest convictions." (Claes Ryn, *America the Virtuous*).

In Africa, where duties previously carried out by other parts of the U.S. government (i.e. building roads and schools) have been transferred to the DoD, a growing American presence is being felt. Fourteen joint-training exercises in eight African nations were held in 2012. One need only examine a list of major oil fields next to a list of U.S. military involvements over the past few years to get an idea of specific Pentagon interests. Deputy commie for EUCOM Lt. General Charles Wald frankly told the *Wall Street Journal* that insuring U.S. access to the huge oil reserves of Nigeria was a key part of AFRICOM's mission (if not for the American people, then at least for U.S.-based multinational energy companies).

Not content to limit the use of drones to Asian countries, the U.S. is making solid drone inroads into Africa. Tiny east African Djibouti was originally the base of choice after 9/11. However, bases located in Ethiopia and the island Seychelles are now reportedly up and buzzing, the latter having been used for missions in nearby Somalia.

In the western African nation of Mali, the U.S. is suffering blowback from its 2011 helping to oust Libya dictator Muammar Gaddafi. Some Gaddafi mercenaries were ethnic Tuaregs, originally from Mali, who picked up Libyan-rebel arms the West had provided and wandered back home to northern Mali. With the aid of an Islamist force, they took over their native (northern) part of the nation, and declared independence. The Islamists then turned on their Tuareg allies and proclaimed Mali an Islamist state. This was all done mere months after a military coup (led by a U.S.-trained captain) had overthrown the democratically elected government. As J.M. Coetzee writes about the Dark Continent, "Gangs of armed men grab power," and then "their activities are respectfully covered in the media — even the western media — under the heading of politics rather than crime."

Naturally, the U.S. now plans to build a drone base in Mali, to monitor Islamists in the region...

---

*   There are still two more "functional" commands — Special Operations Command (SOCOM) and Transportational Command (TRANSCOM).

—February 2013

Chapter Five

Getting One's Wits Back

The presidential primary silly season is upon us. Never one to miss out on the fun is Judge William Whitbeck. The award-winning fiction author displays his talents again ("Faith in America," January 15) by jumping to the defense of Mitt Romney's December 6 address on faith and politics and, concurrently, attacking the heretofore unknown bugbear of Western Civilization – columnist Marianne Means. Means had the audacity to critique the Three Hundred Fifty Million Dollar Man's speech.

Not content with cheering on the Bushmen bludgeoning of America with faith-based social initiatives ($2 million to Nixon ex-con Chuck Colson, $1.5 million to bar exam flunky-turned TV hemorrhoids healer Pat Robertson), faith-based health (the Terri Schiavo fiasco), faith-based science (a National Park Service book now claims the Grand Canyon was formed by Noah's flood), and faith-based war (GWB: "God told me to invade Iraq;" immortal ally Jerry Falwell: "God is pro-war."), Whitbeck skews Means' analysis by stating "Romney is a person of faith and Means is not." How does he know this? Because she states she is not a member of any *organized* religion. Q.E.D.

In a masterly written piece of obfuscation, nowhere does Whitbeck mention 1) the key point of Means' column, or 2) the central tenets of Romney's speech.

Means' point was simply thus: the evangelical portion of the U.S. electorate is the most important element of the GOP coalition - satisfy it, and you've gone a long way to winning the nomination. In 1960, John F. Kennedy had to give a speech to persuade voters he would *not*, as a Catholic, be controlled by a Vatican that had not yet formally renounced American-style democracy (it would soon do so at the Second Vatican Council). Today, Romney has to ease evangelical consciences that are troubled theologically because they believe "his" (i.e. Mormonism's) Jesus is not a member of the divine Trinity. The speech was specifically written for them, and Romney is right in claiming such points of theology are unimportant in political campaigns.

However, to kowtow to this indispensable group, Romney said that those who believe in separation of church and state are "intent on establishing a new religion in America – the religion of secularism." This is code language to many evangelicals; they believe that secularism *is* a religion, despite no evidence other than an inaccurate footnote by Justice Hugo Black in *Torcasco* v *Watkins* (1961), the case that reaffirmed the barring of any religious tests for holding public office. Black claimed "some religions do not believe in God...Secular Humanism and others." From this language, though no one has yet to find a U.S. Secular Humanist church, evangelicals see all the evils of society: women's liberation, gay rights, abortion, evolution, separation of church and state. They've even called Jimmy Carter a secular humanist, though no president knew the Bible better, not to mention taught it as part of his Baptist faith.

Romney also said in his December 6 address at the Bush Library that "freedom requires religion just as religion requires freedom." As Garry Wills has noted, however, "he thus failed to state a fundamental democratic premise: that religious freedom should by definition include the freedom *not* to believe in a religion."

Whitbeck opines that Means didn't read or hear Romney's speech, but inaccurately writes that she called Mitt "an opportunist." Actually, when she wrote that "the press had concluded he was too much of an opportunist, shifting his views to fit the day," Means was referring to Mitt's *father*, George Romney, and his ill-fated 1968 bid for president. (In the interest of full non-disclosure, Whitbeck fails to inform readers he was an aide to Romney *pere* during that time – so perhaps Means has hit a trifle too close to home).

How to survive the silly season, and get one's wit back? Try to forget the past seven years of faith-based government, look historically to the more than 200 years of presidential elections that didn't worry about which candidates paraded their faith like

...remember the founders Jefferson and Madison.

their favorite football teams, and remember the founders Jefferson and Madison. Both formulated magnificent defenses of the separation of church and state. The former is better remembered today. The latter merely wrote the First Amendment. Together they represent not the mythology of Mr. Mitt, but rather our *actual* heritage.

–January 2008

Misappropriating Mr. Madison

> "If Judges interpret the Constitution according to its text, all of the questions are easy, and for the nontextualist, no questions are easy."
>
> **-Justice Antonin Scalia**

Like weeds which overrun a field of wheat, the Federalist Society, now in its 31st year, has spread mightily since its inception. And what better way to have achieved respectability than to use as its emblem a silhouette of revered Founding Father James Madison? Madison, the Greg Maddux of constitutional thinkers, has been used as a club by this right-wing group against its opponents. The Society purports to honor Madison by its ideas.

> "Hee, leading swiftly, Rowld in tangles, and made intricate seem strait."
>
> **-Milton,**
> *Paradise Lost 9.1631-32*

A recurring mantra of this potent cabal (Justice Scalia, Thomas, and Alito are members, Chief Justice Roberts was once listed in its leadership directory) is that judges should use a textual, or "strict constructionist" approach interpreting the Constitution, and not read into it things that are not present. To give a broad interpretation to the document opens the door for mischief, for judicial "activism," as has happened (according to the Society) during the last sixty years.

Again and again, if one explores Madison's actual positions, interesting findings occur. Here are four examples:

1. Federalism – Prior to the Constitution's adoption, our nation went through a period of chaos under the Articles of Confederation. The chief problem of the Articles was its ineffectiveness due to a lack of central authority. Its proponents were concerned with states' sovereignty and feared the loss of states' powers under the new Constitution.

Their concerns were well founded. Madison went to the 1787 Constitutional Convention in Philadelphia to diminish, not defend, the power of the states. His Virginia plan was a virtual blueprint for curbing states' powers. In fact, one of his chief proposals did not pass, as it was deemed too deferential to the national government: "To negative all laws passed by the several states contravening, in the opinion of the national legislature, the articles of Union, and to call forth the force of the union against any member of the union failing to fulfill its duty under the articles thereof." Without this federal veto over state laws, Madison thought, the states would be as uncontrollable as they had been under the Articles.

2. Textualism – In Federalist No. 37 Madison, charged with explaining the Philadelphia Convention's motives, writes, "All new laws, though penned with the greatest technical skill, and passed on the fullest and most mature deliberation, are considered more or less obscure and equivocal, until the meaning be liquidated [clarified] and ascertained by a series of particular discussions and adjudications." He is saying that the Constitution can be better defined by future construing. "A faultless plan was not to be expected," and Madison asks for leniency in judging the Convention's work.

In Federalist No. 44 Madison argues for implied powers. Referring to the "necessary and proper" clause of Section 8 of Article I, regarding congressional powers, Madison writes, "Few parts of the Constitution have been assailed with more intemperance (by the strict constructionists of the day) than this, yes…without the substance of this power, the Constitution would be a dead letter." He argues throughout this paper for the maximum power said phrase will allow.

But it is No. 40 where the Port Conway Concoctor composes his *coup de grace*. Undertaking (some would say conspiring against) the orders of Congress to revise the Articles of Confederation, Madison construes so broadly this call that in fact he obliterates them in their entirety. "The means should be sacrificed to the end;" i.e. forming a new government may have exceeded their authority, but it was warranted to accomplish the peoples' happiness. The skill with which No. 40 is written frustrated the textualists (antifederalists) of the time and its words reverberate throughout our history.

3. *The Judiciary* – Turning to the branch of government which has "increasingly outmuscled the legislature" (former Michigan Supreme Court Chief Justice Cliff Taylor), "run amuck" (Reagan nominated-but-rejected Robert Bork), and whose "tyranny must be ended," (George W. Bush Attorney General John Ashcroft), what is to be done? Bork proposed a constitutional amendment that would allow Congress, by majority vote, to overturn Supreme Court decisions. Contrast this approach with Madison's writing after the Constitutional Convention. He advocated a *stronger* role for the judiciary than what eventually transpired. He proposed a joint judicial/executive veto over congressional legislation. Not getting his way at the Convention in 1788 he suggested, for Kentucky's new state Constitution, an even more active role in legislation for judges than Bork would later denigrate in modern "liberal" courts.

4. *Separation of Church and State* – Tax supported "voucher" initiatives, as well as religious materials at public schools, are both backed by the Society's leading scholars. One sees in these efforts an echo of Patrick Henry's 1785 tax assessment proposal to support religion in general. Henry, arguably the nation's leading *anti*federalist, watched Madison respond with "Memorial and Remonstrance against Religious Assessments." This paper became a classic statement on keeping religion free *from* government, for its own sake. In it Madison argues that civil society can have no jurisdiction over religious faith, and neither can any organ of it.

Those who have problems with the Constitution as a "living" document really have a problem with the original intent of James Madison. The Federalist Society might wish to reconsider changing its emblem to a silhouette of a current Justice, one who has happily contributed to his nation's demise the twin gifts of *Bush v Gore* and *Citizens United*. After all, it is this Justice who says of the Constitution, "I think it's dead," – Antonin "Hammer, Nails, and Coffin" Scalia.*

–February 2013

---

*   Justice Scalia did make the Constitution "come alive" at least once, on June 26, 2008. In order to properly bow to the American Moloch (see 3M Nation), the Reagan appointee wrote the incredibly warped decision of *U.S. v Heller* which, ignoring more than two centuries of legal understanding and rationale, held that the Second Amendment refers to individual gun ownership.

Chapter Six

Down From Buckleyism

Last month's death of William F. Buckley leaves the right-wing mourning the loss of what one historian has observed as "the preeminent voice of modern American conservatism." Buckley is rightly credited with founding the movement, and also with laying the seeds for 1980s Reaganism. Just how far the movement has traveled, and what it meant to begin with, are topics rich with fodder for a curious columnist.

Contrary to myth, *National Review* did not spring forth, in 1955, solely from the head of Buckley, a then not-quite-30 year old writing *wunderkind*. It had a direct ancestry in the old *Freeman* magazines, the first of which was founded in 1920 by Alfred J. Nock, a snobbish friend of Buckley's father. The last of the *Freeman* periodicals died out just as *National Review* was beginning, and the two shared the same printer, stylistic format, and many contributing writers (including several ex-communists). But whereas the *Freeman* looked back to "authentic" liberalism (not to be found in the liberalism of the 1950s), *NR* looked only ahead – and declared Liberalism the Enemy. This was Buckley's stroke of genius.

Buckley spelled out, in *NR's* initial creed, the major policies his thinkers would be grappling with, the first three of which were:

A. "The growth of government must be fought relentlessly. In this great social conflict of the era, we are, without reservations, on the libertarian side."

This was a response to Franklin Roosevelt and Harry Truman's expanding the Federal government during and after World War II, and Dwight Eisenhower's reluctance, in most areas, to scale things backward.

> B. "The profound crisis of our era is the conflict of the Social Engineers, who seek to adjust mankind to conform with scientific utopias, and the disciples of truth, who defend the organic moral order. On this point we are, without reservations, on the conservative side."

This was an attack on Woodrow Wilson-style idealism and its descendants. (Buckley's father, an oilman, was run out of Mexico due to Wilsonian policy there.) The Social Engineers of today are, of course, the neocons, who have attempted to spread utopian democracy at the point of our guns. The results can scarcely have been more disastrous, as even William F. acknowledged in 2006.

> C. "Communism is the No. 1 threat. Coexistence is neither desirable nor possible; we shall oppose any substitute for victory."

Notice the inherent contradiction between points A and C. To stave off the communist threat, America went on a military spending spree unprecedented in history. It is argued by the right-wing that this spending caused the collapse of the Soviet Union, which could not keep up with us, but actual evidence suggests otherwise. The CIA's own estimates of mid-1980's Soviet military spending figures were revised from initially robust 4 to 5 percent annual increases to paltry 1.3 percent enhancements.

A brilliant history teacher at Detroit's Catholic Central High School was the late Frank Garlicki. "The Gar" told his students in the mid-1970s that the Soviet Union was so far behind the U.S. technologically that it faced impending doom, and that it would collapse from within. At least one of his students never forgot his prediction.

What the U.S. received from the arms race were budget deficits so massive that even GOP icon Alan Greenspan now admits that "Reagan borrowed from Clinton" - meaning by

..."Reagan borrowed from Clinton"...

running deficits so unsustainably large it required corrective measures from later Presidents and Congresses.

Buckley's seminal *Up from Liberalism*, published in 1959, took to task middle-of-the-road Dwight Eisenhower and his supposed acquiescence with the prevailing spirit of that age. A half-century later, Eisenhower looks better than ever (certainly better than all his successors), and his farewell address warning of our military-industry complex has proven as prescient as Frank Garlicki's take on Russia. Buckley's great charm and erudite wit could only mask the inherent problems of his original positions. He did demonstrate the capacity to grow, as when he renounced his 1950s defense of segregation. But his ideals long celebrated by some have largely vanished from today's political landscape.

– March 2008

Viva Vidal

Googling YouTube in 2013 and typing in "Buckley Vidal 1968 Conventions," one can find irrefutable proof on celluloid via cyberspace that there was a time when actual debates took place on U.S. public airwaves. The Vietnam War, poverty, social programs, presidential candidates' positions on issues that concerned its citizenry, police state brutality, and the American Empire itself were all topics discussed at the 1968 Republican and Democratic Conventions in 10 to 15 minute uninterrupted segments (or triple the political attention span of latter-day Americans) by two expressively eloquent rivals. It is clear, with 45 years of hindsight, that one of the views expressed would have to be abrogated from political programming, lest viewers begin to understand what the Truman Show is all about.

With William F. Buckley Gore Vidal (1925-2012) shared a birth year, volunteer service in World War II, short stints living in Latin America, unsuccessful campaigns for public office, a prodigious ability to write, and a passionate animosity toward the other (the aforementioned debates led to articles written about them and cross-libel suits filed by each man). Whereas Buckley led a movement, though, Vidal preferred to walk alone, or at least outside the Establishment into which he was very much born (his grandfather had been a U.S. Senator, his father Bureau of Air Commerce head under Franklin Roosevelt). Working this way, Vidal became, in the words of the *Washington Post Book World*, "the master essayist of the age."

Guatemala, which borders Mexico to the south, is where young Gore spent a good deal of 1946. There he saw the workings of U.S. foreign policy up close, and his now forgotten novel *Dark Green, Bright Red* (1950, the year before Buckley was a CIA agent in Mexico) eerily anticipated the real life CIA-led coup of 1954 in that tiny, impoverished nation. In effect, the U.S. overthrew a democratically elected government at the behest of the banana growing United Fruit Company (UFCO).

UFCO owned 42% of Guatemala's land, much of which was unused. To give 100,000 people small plots on which to live and farm, the government moved to appropriate 7% of company-owned land. It offered UFCO $1 million, a figure arrived at based on what the company *claimed the land was worth in its tax returns.* UFCO demanded $16 million. The government refused. The CIA went into action, with MICMAC media dutifully reporting the thwarting of an imminent Soviet Union "beachhead" in Central America. There were, in reality, no ties between Guatemala's president and the Soviets. But the coup was successful. Shortly thereafter, a 36 year civil war ensued, leaving an estimated 200,000 dead.

Vidal's one serious foray into politics was in 1960, when he ran for Congress against an incumbent in a heavily Republican upstate New York district. He lost 57% to 43%, garnering a higher percentage than any Democrat had mastered since 1910, but to his delight ran 20,000 votes ahead of his friend John F. Kennedy there. In *Palimpsest* (Larry McMurtry: "About as good a literary memoir as we have"), Vidal spends a chapter rehashing "Thirteen Green Pages" of notes made contemporaneously with two late August 1961 dates spent with the First Family at their vacation home on Cape Cod, MA (Bobby Kennedy was there as well); a fascinating glimpse of Camelot, with the hindsight of 30-plus years, from a most shrewd and skeptical observer is delivered.

"Narratives of Empire" is Vidal's heptology consisting of *Burr* (1973), *Lincoln* (1984), *1876* (1976), *Empire* (1987), *Hollywood* (1990), *Washington, D.C.* (1967), and *The Golden Age* (2000). These works of historical fiction are remarkable for their size, scope, and attention to detail. Noted critic Harold Bloom wrote that "Vidal's imagination of American politics is so powerful as to compel awe."

The historical novel has been criticized as neither novel nor history, but as Americans have largely ceased to read either history or fiction Vidal's series is an astoundingly good method of (re)introducing oneself to the story of the nation. *Lincoln*, *Empire*, and *The Golden Age* are unequaled manifestations of the genre; the heptalogy as a whole is Condor's answer to his daughters' reverence for the Harry Potter Seven. After a quarter century of reading the version of history produced by "scholar squirrels," -Vidal's term for those professors at U.S. universities whose views must "please their trustees" – "Narratives of Empire" offers a refreshing antidote to the mainstream hagiographies of Great American Leaders.

> **...Vidal's series is an astoundingly good method of (re) introducing oneself to the story of the nation.**

Finally, the ability of a writer to energize his reader's thirst for additional knowledge on his subjects is no small feat. This Vidal did for Condor in *Empire* (Henry Adams, William James) and the title character of *Burr*; Nancy Isenberg's superb later biography of the "Fallen Founder" illuminates in greater depth but is certainly consistent with the Vidalian portrait. Congresswoman Michelle Bachman claims *Burr's* "mocking of the Founding Fathers" turned her from being a liberal Democrat to conservative Republican. Regrettably, her inability to understand what she reads is emblematic of the Tea Party Caucus she founded and chairs.

—March 2013.

Chapter Seven

Shipwrecked

What has just happened? I refer not to the recent presidential election but rather the electoral cycle itself-a two-year 24/7 mind-numbing suck-us-in process that made morbid addicts of many mild-mannered political aficionados who collectively wondered what Chuck Todd or Chris Matthews or Bill Schneider or George Stephanopoulos or the feckless folks at Fox would have for us next in attempted analysis and spin. Throughout the 17,000 hours and millions of sound bites entering our consciousness, could there have been a hidden purpose behind it all?

A pecuniary statistic suggests that there was. Stunning info released right before November 4 revealed six billion dollars has been spent on the presidential and congressional campaigns, much of it for advertising on the same networks owned by the very corporations that, neatly, influence the elected officials-a near perfectly corrupt system with no end in sight. Indeed, our Emeritus Essayist-in-Chief Gore Vidal may have to sequel *Perpetual War for Perpetual Peace* with *Perpetual Campaigns for Perpetual Non-governance* (Sarah 2012 began *before* her ignominious defeat with the Aged Rebel).

Earlier in the season, a local jurist ordered, at an event centered upon the unlikely but ultimately successful unseating of a state Supreme Court chief justice, his usual current concoction of Captain and cranberry. What in blazes do you call it, inquired Wayne County's top political strategist? Momentary inspiration occurred. "A Shipwreck," was the response. Ah, a drink for the times...

Comical cries on the right warn of impending socialism. What we have witnessed over the past 30 years is redistributionism of a different kind. In 1978, the top one percent wealthiest Americans owned 20% of the wealth. Today it's 40%. Socialism for the ultra-rich was not accomplished without a plan. In fact, its roots may be traced to a little remembered Supreme Court case of the 19th Century.

The 14th Amendment was enacted in 1868 to give African-Americans first-class citizenship. In two Federal Court cases before 1886, judges ruled that the Amendment's Equal Protection Clause protecting "persons" was not, obviously, meant to include corporations. Nonetheless, in *Santa Clara County v. Southern Pacific Railroad* (1886), the U.S. Supremes, before ruling that a county's tax on a railroad was void for other reasons, stated that it "did not wish to hear argument on the question" of whether corporations were protected by the Equal Protection Clause because "we are all of the opinion that they are."

..."we are all of the opinion that they are."

Later, in *Connecticut General Life Insurance v Johnson* (1938), the 14th's Due Process Clause was used to protect these "persons." Justice William O. Douglas observed, "The corporations already had the sword of financial power, the famous American names, the big prestige behind them. Now they had the shield of the Constitution."

The sword and shield have served Corporate America well, and the plundering continues to the present day. Infamous mercenary outfit Blackwater recently use the Due Process Clause successfully (in U.S. District Court) to thwart the City of San Diego's efforts to keep a training facility out of its area. And many industries are now racing to grab onto Treasury Secretary Hank Paulson's $700 billion taxpayer-funded bag of goodies. As our $10 trillion public debt rises, the experimental fiscal policies of Reagan/Bush I/Bush II come to rotten fruition. But wait....in the sky, above

MARK J. PLAWECKI

the clouds, the jet-propelled rescue squad of...Air Obama! Can it reach us stranded islanders in time, or will January 20th be too late? And will it have We the People's interests at heart, or have the multinationals purchased another one?

—November 2008

Still Stranded

"The court does not wish to hear argument on the question whether the provision in the 14th Amendment to the Constitution, which forbids a state to deny to any person within its jurisdiction the equal protection of the laws, applies to those corporations. We are all of the opinion that it does."

The above words are attributed to U.S. Supreme Court Chief Justice Morrison R. Waite in the aforementioned 1886 *Santa Clara County* v *Southern Pacific Railroad* case. What Condor didn't realize in 2008, but learned after reading Thom Hartmann's book *Unequal Protection* (2010), was that this quote appears not in the body of the decision but rather in the court reporter's *head note,* and thus had no legal precedential value or indeed any legal standing at all. Additionally, Waite allegedly made the statement fifteen months *after* the case had been argued (in January 1885) and moments before he turned to Associate Justice John M. Harlan to read the court's opinion of May 10, 1886.

How could/did this happen? Hartmann's research shows that court reporter J. Bancroft Davis, a Harvard-educated lawyer and former railroad company president involved in several prominent legal actions of his era, simply at a later time added that language himself. (Supreme Court reporters of this period earned, with the royalties from writing the *United States Reports,* more money than the justices for whom they worked.)

Letters unearthed between Waite and Davis, from after the decision was announced, indicate the latter *was* in fact given some leeway to comment in the head note about the Court's *internal* debate of the corporate personhood question. However, Waite's correspondence also included the language, "inasmuch as we *avoided* meeting the constitutional question in the decision," clearly indicating the issue was not part of the result reached.

In other words, the Supreme Court of the United States, contrary to universal belief and later derived-from case law, never actually *ruled* that corporations are persons. Through Davis's mistake, or deliberate scheme (as some researchers believe, since there was one Justice, Stephan J. Field, who had previously ruled as a Ninth Circuit Judge that corporations *were* persons, and may have influenced Davis to write the head note which conveniently mirrored Field's previous lower court language), they simply became persons. And their enormous strength only continues to grow.

How much so? To Google "Obama is a socialist" yields 29,700,000 results (in .16 seconds). Though Sarah 2012 fizzled early, perhaps because few voters (even Republicans) thought Ms. Palin qualified to visit, let alone labor as an occupant of, the Oval Office, these facts did not prevent corporate Fox "News" from paying her $1 million per annum for enlightened commentary. One such on-air insight delivered in December 2012 was her stated belief in Obama's socialism; later that month Peter Ferrara in the corporate magazine *Forbes* claimed the President was a Marxist.

A check of that most obtrusive of right wing annoyances-the record-reveals that under Obama's first four socialist/Marxist years, corporate profits increased 171%, more than under Leninists Reagan, Bush I, Bush II, Taft, Harding, Calvin "The business of America is business" Coolidge, or any other administration since 1900. Did said profits profit the American worker? One study reported in the *Wall Street Journal* showed that 93% of 2009-10 income growth went to the top 1% clearly too unfair to the non-Ninety-nines for Fox and *Forbes*.

Another striking analysis was conducted by the Associated Press in January 2013.* It showed that from 2007 to mid-2009 (when the Great Recession officially ended), 7.5 million jobs were lost. Of them, half paid "middle class wages," defined from $38,000 to $68,000. Since the recession's end, 3.5 million jobs have been added. This is most troubling in itself, since rebounds from prior recessions have never failed to gain back all jobs within three years.

But the most frightening news is not the meager number of jobs gained, disheartening as that is. The AP study found that of the newly created 3.5 million jobs, 29% pay *above* $68,000, and 69% pay *below* $38,000. That leaves 2% for the former mid-pay jobs. And thanks to technology, these positions are not coming back. The American middle class is essentially vehicled on the road to oblivion.

As for Paulsen's infamous $700 billion Bag of Goodies, less noted now is the $16.1 *trillion* loaned from the U.S. to the giant banks, some of which were foreign. Nearly half the total went to perennial trick-or-treaters Citibank, Morgan Stanley, Merrill Lynch, and Bank of America. Needless to say, the loans were at or near zero percent, so the banks could borrow at that rate and invest at a higher one –their one steady stream of revenue.

Thus it turns out that Air Obama's rescue jet was piloted by corporate CEOs, and owned by Corporate Airlines. Not only is it not about to rescue the 90%-plus of Americans stranded on the Island of Misfit Girls and Boys, it has flown to a safe tax haven island of its own. If only the Bermuda Triangle could produce its mythical magic on these high flyers of fabulous finance.

–March 2013

---

* "The Great Reset: Disappearing Jobs," *The Detroit Legal News*, January 23, 2013.

Chapter Eight

The Disconnect

There are an increasing number of learned people who claim Barack Obama will take office under the worst conditions since the Great Depression. These folks are probably too sanguine. One must go back to 1861 when Abraham Lincoln faced seven seceded states (four more would soon follow) to find a more daunting challenge to an incoming American administration.

Consider. The public and private debt of this nation now exceeds $50 *trillion*. This staggering figure must be placed in context. It represents 3.5 times our annual gross domestic product. The last Depression bottomed out in 1933 with a 3.35 ratio of debt-to-GDP. And we are nowhere near bottom. November's unemployment numbers were frightening-533,000 new job losses, or 173,000 more than expected. Despite $6.3 trillion, by *Forbes'* estimate, being injected into the private sector by the Federal Reserve and the Treasury, banks are not lending to each other or other borrowers. The system is paralyzed.

Why hasn't the massive liquidity increase helped? Because sophisticated financial instruments known as credit derivatives, of which the most prominent is the credit default swap, have been unregulated (by a law passed by Congress in 2000); $62 trillion is involved here. Credit default swaps are insurance-like agreements between large financial institutions, except one need not own the underlying asset nor suffer a loss to recover. Geniuses at J.P. Morgan Chase thought up this concept in 1997; excessive leverage was the result. Senator Carl Levin stated on December 4 that the Big Three automakers alone were into these instruments to the tune of "hundreds of billions" of dollars. As the instruments unravel (like a giant Ponzi scheme, exactly what a former Nasdaq chairman was just indicted of -$50 billion was bilked there), this house of cards collapses.

Unfortunately, another critical problem the nation faces goes perpetually unnoticed. Congress, which ceded spending oversight authority to the Pentagon some time ago, gives zero indication it wishes to reign in the largest part of our discretionary budget. Forty-eight percent of the world's military budget is ours, money spent to provide us an army with fewer troop units, navy with fewer ships, and air force with fewer working planes than at any time since World War II. The waste and fraud in Iraq (separated here from the waste and fraud of the War itself) has been egregious, yet nothing is done to reduce or even expose the situation.

The crystallization of this phenomenon was perfected on September 25th. The day before, the House had passed, by a 370-58 margin, a $630 billion spending bill in which virtually no debate occurred. On the 25th the nation's print media, from the hallowed *New York Times* on downward, made no, or next-to-no, mention of what the bill contained.

The *Detroit Free Press*, supposedly the more *liberal* of the two metro Detroit dailies, strategically placed on the bottom of page four a story entitled "GOP gets energy policy win as House backs offshore drilling," a classic case of treating the margin as text. Not a one of the 221-word story (yes, I counted) stated what the money was actually going *for*, much to the delight of our Pentagon owners. By not reporting that this behemoth spends $1 trillion per year (30% more than the initial Wall Street bailout), we need never be bothered by *how* it's spent.

Neither, of course, does the Pentagon. On September 10, 2001, then-Secretary of Defense Donald Rumsfeld spoke of how $2.3 trillion was *unaccounted for* by Pentagon bookkeepers; something happened

... $2.3 trillion was *unaccounted for* by Pentagon bookeepers...

the next day which made us all forget this fact. Nor does the institution even receive yearly audits-though it is promising to get one by 2015 (imagine if you or I had such a luxury for the next six years).*

But fear not. Change is coming. Robert Gates, a man so clueless as deputy CIA director in the late 1980s that he saw not the impending collapse of the Soviet Union and was so tied to the Iran-Contra scandal that he could not be confirmed CIA director in 1987 (although Congress forgot about the scandal four years later when it did confirm him) will be Obama's Defense Secretary. Presumably the President-elect will guide him in a different direction than did Gates' current boss, the forever-to-be remembered gift to satire George W. Bush.** After all, this is why the modern Man from Illinois was elected, *n'est-ce-pas?*

-December 2008

---

* Congress passed a law in 2009 ordering the Pentagon to be audit-ready by 2017. Bettors of that actually happening are also rumored to be predicting the Detroit Lions will win the Super Bowl in 2015.

** He didn't. Gates served as Defense Secretary for 2 ½ years, then wrote a memoir sharply criticizing Obama for not being enthusiastic enough about the Afghanistan war. Perhaps using himself as a reverse barometer, Gates stated he wanted "to write a book on how to successfully reform and change public institutions."

Condor's Corollary

Desire appears to be, according to Rene Girard, the fundamental individual prerogative. But this noted cultural critic, who increasingly gains converts as thinking humans contemplate the world's current dilemma, claims (in a spectacular body of work) that we gave up this fundamental prerogative at the very dawn of our species. In fact, imitative, or *mimetic* desire, is what makes us distinct from the animals we evolved from but, though it is our basic trait, it's one we don't realize. We borrow our desires from others. Desire is, in a paradoxical way, always wanting to be "the other."

Unlike Sigmund Freud, who postulated that man's desires are instinctual and run counter to society's norms, and so he must learn to repress them (i.e. he believed the male child's instinct is to replace his father so as to possess his mother), Gerard sees desire in an imitative triangular formation. There is a lack in all of us of knowing what we want, so we latch onto a model who desires a certain object, and we then imitate this model. (Modern advertising is unquestionably based on this concept.) Girard's analysis of a litany of literature's great authors found that they understood, intuitively or through experience, this triangular nature of desire.

Girard's theory was certainly controversial when first presented in *Deceit, Desire, and the Novel* (1961), but it has slowly and steadily gained traction, and now has the backing of empirical research-neuroscientists have found "mirror neurons" used by babies less than a month old so that imitation of others (typically parents) can be explained as the biological phenomenon of the initial learning process.

Mimetic theory explains our actions and habits in many ways. James Carroll, well acquainted with Girardian thought, writes that "the inbuilt restlessness of human incompleteness is channeled into the will to consume and acquire, fueling the illusion that the restlessness can be quieted by satisfaction of the next desire."

Nowhere has the will (not to mention the ability) to "consume and acquire" reached a higher plateau in man's history than in post-World War II America. Andrew Bacevich has insightfully suggested a sacred trinity of U.S. foreign policy convictions as "Global military presence, global power projection, and global interventionism." To the Bacevich Trinity a Condor Corollary sacred trio of percentages might be helpfully added. For 2011, these three percentages were "4.6/24/41" where

- 4.6 was the U.S. share of world population
- 24 was the U.S. share of world use of natural resources
- 41 was the U.S. share of world military spending.

A poll taken in July 2012 showed that more than 75% of Americans, when explained options and given both for and against arguments, prefer our gargantuan military budget cut. Though not informed (in this poll nor anywhere else in corporate media) that we spend virtually tenfold on our defense per capita vis-à-vis the world, the average American's instincts (or perhaps desires) to set common sense priorities when say, Detroit is about to go bankrupt, are encouraging.

Unfortunately, the view among the MICMAC elites who control federal purse strings is almost unanimously opposed to such cuts. Why?

MICMAC has been brilliant in spreading defense contracts to companies in *all 435* congressional districts. In fact, a comfortable majority of districts (270) have garnered at least $1 billion in contracts over the years 2000-2012. The not completed F-35 combat aircraft alone uses 1300 suppliers in 45 states, and with the Air Force, Marines, and Navy all due to duplicate having it, the cost over its lifetime is projected to be $1.4 trillion (don't be too concerned about this projection's accuracy though- the F-35 is already 75% over budget).

Eisenhower's words quoted above were spoken in the early stages of the Cold War. The mimetic rivalry between the U.S. and Soviet Union can be seen in the escalation of nuclear weapons. The U.S. had 1005 when Eisenhower's speech was made, the Soviet Union 50. Eventually our nuclear stockpile grew to a high of 31,700 (in 1966); the Soviets eventually surpassed the U.S. in quantity by 1978. The U.S.S.R. numbers peaked at 40,723 in 1986, a mere five years before it ceased to exist. Together the two superpowers built over 100,000 nukes during the course of the Cold War, or as Carroll puts it, "Hiroshima raised to infinity."

In today's *non*-nuclear market, there appears but a remnant of the former rivalry. While it's true the U.S. and Russia rank #1 and #2 in the Arms Sold to Other Nations Olympics, the 2011 totals demonstrate the evil ex-Reds have some catching up to do. Russia sold 5.6% of all military weapons, earning a silver to co-evil current Red China's bronze (2.5% share). However, chants of "USA! USA!" could be heard throughout the corridors of Lockheed Martin and Boeing, as the home country won the gold with an impressive 78% share of the $85.3 billion market to insure "peace and stability" throughout the world.

-March 2013

Chapter Nine

The Lions in Winter

In a heretofore unnoticed coincidence of some little amusement, the dual performances of U.S. presidents and those of the Detroit Lions have historically mirrored each other to an uncanny degree. We begin this exercise in frivolity at the point of the football franchise's transfer, from Portsmouth to Detroit, in 1934 (or Year XXXIII B.S. – in NFLspeak, Before Superbowl). Records and/or Lions win percentages are noted for each administration.

Firstly must be mentioned our Augustus, Franklin Roosevelt, who held the Mr. President title as if gained by birthright which, in a sense, he had. The initial *Lion* title arrived in 1935, during the high water mark of activity known as FDR's first term. The eleven year record of the team (1934-1944) in Roosevelt's time was 63-54-6 (.537), pretty solid numbers despite a desultory 0-11 1942 squad, when the U.S. was taking its lumps in the Pacific following Pearl Harbor.

Harry S Truman presided next. A 7-3 Lion mark in 1945 (HST and FDR holdovers lead us to a victory in World War II) sadly was not a portent of seasons to come. Detroit went 32-50-1 from 1946-1952 (.392), years when Old Harry permanently militarized the nation in such a way that today's Pentagon Overlordship goes mostly unnoticed by zombie-like citizens (recent U.S. adult basic civics test score average: 49%). We've yet to pay the bill for this borrowed inheritance, but sooner rather than later will.

After Americans sensibly drove Truman back to his native Missouri, they turned to the one ruler of the 20th century who had presidential stature *before* he occupied the Oval Office: Dwight D.

Eisenhower. The Lions, upon news of Ike's 1952 election, promptly won their second NFL championship. Two more (in 1953 and 1957) would be nabbed during the DDE years. Unsurprisingly, Ike turned out to be the best president we've had since World War II; he ended the Korean debacle, instituted the Interstate Highway Act, and kept us in relative peace and prosperity.

The cold, calculating, charismatic John F. Kennedy (1961-1963) followed Eisenhower. A .618 Lions win percentage, their highest under any president, nicely corresponds with the last White House tenant who could, for all his flaws, be objectively judged "good." Mediocrities and mountebanks were to follow JFK; for Lions' fans, the fact that William Clay Ford chose the date of November 22, 1963 to purchase their favorite franchise, pretty much summarizes the next 45 years.

Lyndon Johnson's (.425) courage and can-do attitude on civil rights must regrettably be outweighed by his tragic escalation of Vietnam's virtual destruction. Richard Nixon (.600), the exception who proves the rule, was driven from office rather than face certain impeachment and likely conviction. He must be credited, however, with openings to China and the Soviet Union, our previously mortal and godless enemies, so he proved also the maxim that there is some good in every man.

The profoundly decent, but just as profoundly inadequate caretakers Gerald Ford (.476) and Jimmy Carter (.414) finished off the 1970s. The Peanut Man's "malaise" speech in 1979 presaged a 2-14 gridiron disaster for Our Cleated Heroes that fall. Carter gave us in turn the amiable Ronald Reagan (.379), still titan to those zealots who insist, with Dick Cheney, that balancing the nation's checkbook is for sissies. Midway through the Gipper's two-term fiasco, the U.S. became a debtor country for the first time since 1914; the four worst deficits since Hiroshima were Ronnie's, too, until the current CEO decided to end *his* eight years with a deluge of red ink no ocean including the Pacific could contain.

The first George Bush (.469) had, in an otherwise lackluster regime, one shining success – the 1991 genuinely coalition - led driving from Kuwait of Saddam Hussein. The Lions, for the only time during Ford's tenure, made it to the NFC title game that year.

Eight years of foibles and missteps collectively known as the Clinton Era ensued, though it can be reasonably

...closer than any Kennedy successor to receiving an above average grade.

argued that Cigar Bill (.515, five playoff appearances) came closer than any Kennedy successor to receiving an above average grade. His administration did achieve three annual surpluses. Unfortunately, they resulted from the fraudulent accounting gimmick of using the Social Security and Medicare Trust Funds to mask actual, if admittedly more manageable, deficits.

Which brings us to our hapless Romulus Augustus, G.W. Bush (.242), dizzying accelerator of the national decline, and so effective in this apparently self-appointed task that even the zombies are awakening. The 0-16 Lion "perfection" of 2008, following seven prior losing seasons under Bush, fits perfectly with the worst financial collapse since Herbert Hoover and Portsmouth. He also bequeaths us two ongoing wars of choice and, as a bonus, ends his career as he started it at Phillips Academy, as head cheerleader.

But instead of touchdowns and field goals, Bush rides into his (and our) sunset cheering on bombs and tanks delivered into Gaza. Fortunately, we are assured by the invading nation's foreign minister that there is "no humanitarian crisis in Gaza." Otherwise, we might mistakenly misconstrue a muted military maneuver for a malthusian massacre.

And so Suetonius, chronicler of *The Twelve Caesars*, sends a message from the dustbin of history: "Good luck, Mr.

President-elect, even with new draft choices, in transforming your 0-16 roster of professionals. You might, in a kindly yet persuasive way, wish to ask Mr. Ford if he's ready to sell yet."

Longtime zombie Mark J. Plawecki serves on the 20th District Court bench in Dearborn Heights.

-January 2009

Grading the Prof

Four winters hence, Ford has not sold, the Lions have gone 22-42 (.344)* and, according to the theory, Barack Obama's first term places him on pace to become the second worst president of the Nuclear Era. Can such a case be plausibly made? Before it is discussed, one Former President Update must be mentioned.

The central national event hovering over Condor's youth was the Kennedy Assassination. Might Have Been is usually dull sport, but in this case the seminal query of What Would JFK Have Done in Vietnam, speculative by nature, can be profitably pondered. Gordon M. Goldstein's excellent and revealing *Lessons in Disaster: McGeorge Bundy and the Path to War in Vietnam* (2008) provides clear and convincing evidence that Kennedy, who until the time of his death had refused to send combat troops to Southeast Asia, would not have done so had he lived.

Bundy, the national security adviser to both Kennedy and Lyndon Johnson, was the legendary epitome of the so-called "Best and Brightest" crew with whom Kennedy had surrounded himself. He was collaborating with Goldstein on what was to be a mea culpa book when he died of a massive heart attack in 1996. His notes reflect an October 2, 1963 meeting with Kennedy, Secretary of Defense Robert McNamara, and General Maxwell Taylor where JFK had decided (against Bundy's judgment) to withdraw 1000 of the then 16,000 military "advisers" in Vietnam, with the rest to be withdrawn by the end of 1965.

Kennedy had stood up to Pentagon pressure before, in the Bay of Pigs fiasco and the Cuban Missile Crisis. Hawks surrounding him in both cases wanted American bombs to rain on Cuba. Contrast his performance with that of Barack Obama.

In late 2009 Obama received a Pentagon report recommending a troop surge in Afghanistan, which advised using the classic "clear and hold" strategy of expelling insurgents from key geographic areas. First promulgated in modern times by the British in 1948 in Malaya, this approach was virtually copied by the U.S. under LBJ in Vietnam with the infamous Strategic Hamlet program. However, the historically challenged first year president had neither the wisdom nor courage to overrule MICMAC demands, and the tragic contributing blunder to the now longest war in U.S. annals, wearily slogs onward.

Failure to reign in, by mere tinkering with, the American Empire earns Obama a "C" grade in this subject. It is but one of four major areas in which the former constitutional law professor needs to be graded. The other three are preservation of the Constitution (with his background, Obama would seem to have an advantage in this class), the economy, and the ecology (which just might need to be more than tinkered with if posterity is to survive).

The Presidential oath of office affirms that the oath taker will "preserve, protect, and defend" the U.S. Constitution. During his first term, Barack Obama has

- Prosecuted more whistleblowers under the Espionage Act than all previous presidents combined – after promising a transparent government
- Taken the position that the U.S. government can kill by drone U.S. citizens who "an informed high-level official" of said government determines is an imminent threat to the U.S.-thereby negating the deprivation of "life, liberty, or property, without due process of law" clause of the 5th Amendment
- Waged an illegal (non-declared by Congress) war in Libya, creating blowback in Mali

- Conducted innumerable warrantless searches against U.S. citizens, rendering the 4th Amendment inoperative.

For Constitutional protection Obama earns a "D."

Turning to the economy, the financialization of which was firmly entrenched by the time Obama took office, it was obvious to nearly all that its 2008 near-collapse was caused by just this phenomenon. Like Franklin Roosevelt in 1933, Obama had an opportunity to structurally change the way Wall Street steals from everyone else while Washington gives it legal sanction. Instead, the rookie president turned to the *very people* who contributed to the meltdown– Timothy Geithner and Lawrence Summers and numerous other Robert Rubin protégés whose Wring No Actual Concessions from Wall Street approach led to today's institutionalized corporate welfare. Bloomberg reported (February 20, 2013) that without taxpayer subsidies effectively amounting to $83 billion per year ($64 billion to the five largest) these banks would barely be profitable. With the U.S. unemployment rate the same (7.9%) in January 2013 as it was in January 2009, Obama earns a "C" in Economics class..

Ecology– On the positive side, the blocking of the XL Pipeline (at least until now) which would spell emissions disaster for the planet, and improved auto fuel efficiency standards have been achieved. Unfortunately, little else was done. If climate change were a normal issue, Obama's balanced approach might seem reasonable. It is, however, unlike any mankind has faced, and the President's virtual four year silence when he had the World's No.1 Bully Pulpit has done irreparable damage. Obama gets a political "C" in this area,

> **Instead, the rookie president turned to the *very people* who contributed to the meltdown**

though as Bill McKibben often points out, physics and chemistry do not care a whit for what politicians think is doable or reasonable.

Did Obama break the Mediocrities and Mountebanks streak? A 1.75 GPA in the four core subjects suggests that he hasn't-yet. In fairness, he has faced a degree of hostility from MICMAC that no president before him ever had to. Perhaps, given the present power structure, the streak is unbreakable. But it would be inspirational indeed if someone actually made the attempt.

—March 2013

---

*   Now 29-51 (.363) through 2013.

Chapter Ten

Whither Special Relationships?

Garry Wills' take on pre-Vatican II Catholicism might be more appropriately applied to current U.S. relations with Israel. During the recent twenty-two day blitzkrieg launched into Gaza, which mainstream media euphemistically called a "war" (the sides pitted against one another were akin to the 2008 Divine Child 6th grade baseball team vs. the Philadelphia Phillies), roughly 1300 Gazans were killed (along with 4500 wounded), most of them civilians. Thirteen Israelis also died, four by friendly fire.

On the fourteenth day of the carnage, the United Nations' Security Counsel proposed a cease-fire resolution that was generated by U.S. Secretary of State Condoleezza Rice. The vote was expected to be 15-0 in favor, reflecting the world's horror at what was happening. But it turned out to be 14-0, with one abstention. Here is what Reuters reported, verbatim, of Israeli Prime Minister Ehud Olmert's remarks during a January 12 press conference:

> When we saw that the Secretary of State, for reasons we did not really understand, wanted to vote in favor of the U.N. resolution... I looked for President Bush and they told me he was in Philadelphia making a speech.

I said 'I don't care. I have to talk to him now.' They got him off the podium, brought him to another room and I spoke to him. I told him, 'You can't vote in favor of this resolution.' He said, 'Listen, I don't know about it. I didn't see it. I'm not familiar with the phrasing.' I said, 'I'm familiar with it. You can't vote in favor.'

He gave an order to Rice and she did not vote in favor of it-a resolution she cooked up, phrased, organized and maneuvered for. She was left shamed and abstained on a resolution she arranged.

These comments were noted throughout the globe, with the conspicuous exception of the press from the country that abstained from the cease-fire resolution. That country was the United States.

Now, Condor has not graduated from the reportedly excellent Brian Sullivan* School of Logic, but he believes there are but two choices here. Either Olmert told the truth, wherein Hebrew should soon be made mandatory in our public schools, or he lied. And if he lied, then why has the U.S. media kept silent about his, to say the least, *embarrassing* allegations? For the record, the U.S. State Department called Olmert's version of events "100 percent, totally, completely untrue."

Exactly one month after the Security Council vote, Barack Obama held his first formal presidential press conference. Helen Thomas asked him, "Do you know of any country in the Middle East that has nuclear weapons?" Obama responded:

With respect to nuclear weapons, you know, I don't want to speculate. What I know is this: that if we see a nuclear arms race in a region as volatile as the Middle East, everybody will be in danger.

Actually, the rookie President knows a great deal more than he portends. He knows, for example, what every other leader (and many others) on the planet knows: that Israel is a long -time nuclear power, with a stockpile of at least 100 deliverable warheads. This fact is also kept hidden from the American people, who are taught to "know" only that "madmen" from Iran are "on the verge" of acquiring their first nukes.

A curious state of silence, then, accentuates this very special relationship. It completely contradicts the Farewell Address of an ancient regime, now alien to us, which warned that "a passionate attachment of one nation for another produces a variety of evils." That Address stated that such an attachment bequeaths the former the "wars and quarrels of the latter" and is "particularly alarming to the truly enlightened and independent Patriot."

The regime referred to is that of the first U.S. President. What Americans are supposed to now think of this man hasn't been made clear to us by our purveyors of information. However, a minor middle-aged jurist with a mediocre memory can recall at least one lesson from his delusional youth: this fellow, named Washington, was to be revered, for as long as it lasted, as the Father of His Country.

−February 2009

---

*   A notably bright legal mind who serves on the Third Circuit Court bench in Wayne County, MI.

2 + 2 = ?

On March 4, 2013 Vice President Joe Biden addressed 13,000 friendly American Israel Public Affairs Committee (AIPAC) members and supporters in Washington, D.C. He pledged that the United States was "not bluffing" when it stated it would intervene militarily, if necessary, to prevent Iran from developing a nuclear weapon. He also said that Iran's "dangerous nuclear weapons program" not only endangers "Israel, but endanger(s) the world."

The speech was a virtual replay of his 2009 address before the same body, complete with his heartfelt story of how as a young U.S. Senator in 1973 (Biden was 30 when elected the year before) he travelled to Israel and had the high honor of meeting Israeli Prime Minister Golda Meir. He touchingly recounted how Meir read him letter after letter from Israelis who had suffered and/or lost loved ones in 1967's Six Day War, and that he found himself shaken by the grave situation Israel seemed to be in. Then, however, the Prime Minister had stiffened his resolve by telling him that Israel had a secret weapon. "Our secret weapon, Senator, is that we have no place else to go."

The State of Israel actually had another secret weapon at the time, and it factors prominently in one of the most astonishing, if vastly underreported events, of the Cold War Era. Shortly after Biden's 1973 visit to Israel, the Yom Kippur War ensued. This war began with Syria and Egypt jointly attacking Israel on the holiest day of the Jewish calendar, and for several days following they appeared ready to deliver a knockout blow. Israeli defense minister Moshe Dayan in fact stated "This is the end of the Third Temple," with the first being the one the Babylonians destroyed in 587 BCE, and the second that the Romans did likewise to in 70CE.

It was precisely at this pivotal moment in the tiny nation's history that Meir ordered the arming of the "Temple Weapons," the nuclear missiles that Israel had secretly built over the previous decade-and-a-half (to this day officially unacknowledged by Israel), and unmistakably pointed them at the Syrian and Egyptian cities of Damascus and Cairo. This time, the Israelis were saying, there would be no second Holocaust without the taking down of their enemies. "The Samson Option," so named for the Biblical person whose suicide also destroyed his foes, thus was unveiled.

Short of Samson, Israel at this point felt that only U.S. intervention could stop the Arab momentum. Its ambassador informed U.S. Secretary of State Henry Kissinger that if the Americans did not resupply the Israeli military with weaponry (including previously embargoed antitank missiles that had been banned by Congress to sell to Israel), the embattled Mideast nation would be "going nuclear." Kissinger was horrified, but almost immediately began to shift U.S. weaponry stationed in Europe to resupply the Israeli military. The Israeli threat had succeeded. (It should be noted that President Nixon was in the throes of the Watergate scandal during this period, and had virtually ceased functioning as Commander in Chief.)

So Biden neglected, or perhaps remains blissfully ignorant of, this part of the 1973 story about our "great friend and ally." Faced with possible destruction, Israel acted as probably any other government in its place would have done. Yet it remains amazing that, unlike the Cuban Missile Crisis of 1962, which is etched in the collective global memory as the nearest we've come to nuclear war, the Yom Kippur war event is known, even today, by next to no one.*

> ...the Yom Kippur war event is known, even today, by next to no one.

One month before the Vice President's speech to AIPAC, a Gallup poll found 99% of Americans surveyed considered Iran's potential development of nuclear weapons a critical or important threat to the United States. No polls can be found as to what percentage perceive Israel a threat. None, to Condor's knowledge, have ever been conducted. Nuclear blackmail pays rather well.

MICMAC math can be summed as follows:

1. Iran — No nukes + no evidence that it is working to develop nukes (according to both U.S. and Israeli intelligence) = an existential threat to the world
2. North Korea — Nuclear weapons + threatening to use their weapons on America (March 7, 2013) = no existential threat

Or, as Orwell wrote in *1984*, $2 + 2 = 5$

In the 2012 presidential debate on foreign policy, Iran was mentioned 47 times, Israel 34, North Korea 1, Palestine zero. Since the entire raison d'être of Israel's neighbor problems stems from its treatment of the occupied Palestinian territories, it is indeed masterful that no mention is made of it and next-to-no mention made of nuclear wielding North Korea. Such framing of correct questions represents MICMAC at it finest.

---

*   This account of the Yom Kippur War borrows heavily from James Carroll, *Jerusalem, Jerusalem*, p. 278-284 and Seymour Hersh, *The Samson Option*, p. 222-226.

−April 2013

Chapter Eleven

A Thousand Points of "Light"

For this column Condor is joined by predecessor Spartacus and their erstwhile pal Boethius. The Scene: Bankrupt America's epicenter, Detroit, MI. The Time: The St. Patrick's Day celebrations of Mid-March, 2009. All dialogue is genuine.

Sparty: What was the trip-'em-up question again?

Condor: How many bases does the U.S. military have in foreign countries?

Bo: Why ask the people interested in becoming governor of a slowly-being-evacuated Midwest industrial state?

Condor: OK, they're not running for a job in Washington. But doesn't this type of person, unless born in Canada, become an immediately plausible national candidate?

Bo: True enough. Plus our working thesis is "If these folks have no idea, how can the rest of us Joseph and Josephine Six-packs have a clue?

Condor: Let's get to work. There's our first victim. The always cerebral Andy "Job Killin" Dillon. Mr. Speaker, what's your guess as to the number of bases?

Dillon: I'd say about one hundred.

Sparty: Nice try, Double Domer. But we'll move on.

Condor: Next, I see the always amiable John "Drop the Lieutenant" Cherry. Governor?

Cherry: I'd guess forty.

Sparty: We're on a roll. And much in luck, 'cause ten feet away campaigns the always congenial Mike "(Sub)urban legend" Cox. A former marine, he's the betting favorite for getting this right. General, what say you?

Cox: One hundred twenty. No, let me revise that. One hundred eighty.

Condor: Thank you, General. Presently, we're caught in the food queue following Mass at Most Holy Trinity...

Sparty: Where our next unsuspecting victim, from parts out West, is Terri "Grand(ville)" Land.* Madame Secretary?

Land: In excess of one hundred.

Sparty: Care to be more specific?

Land: No. And I'll thank you not to steal the potatoes from my plate. Also, please stop pestering me about the 1977 Grandville hoops squad that lost to Divine Child.

Condor: We could have been more diplomatic there, guys.

Bo: Seen one too many Skubick Ambushes on *Off the Record.*

Sparty: Hey, there's Brooks "Bring Back (Limo) Busing" Patterson! Fearlessly campaigning in Coleman's Cass Corridor. Mr. County Exec?

Patterson: Thirty-two. No wait, that's Valentina's age. Then I'll say twenty-five.

Condor: Ouch. Those answers might cause him to become the first dropout from the race (Editor's note: They did)

Bo: Finally, we catch up with a candidate from Mr. Peabody's Wayback Machine, David Plawecki.

Condor: Wasn't Cousin David the youngest senator (age 22) in state history? Of whom it was once written, "Spends more time at his desk working than any other two legislators put together?"

Sparty: That's no way to get elected. Anyway, in The Family, the new granddad is known as Slow Bro to Fast Eddie and Slick Rick.

Bo: Mr. P, no one's yet come close. Can you enlighten us?

Plawecki: Five thousand, Sherman.

Sparty: Whoa! Gramps must be confusing my question with how many vacation trips he's planned since retirement.

Condor: Folks, that concludes the survey. What's the correct answer, Bo?

Bo: The men in the Pentagon suits admit to 865. That's bases *outside the United States.* But they don't count those in Iraq or Afghanistan. The true number, carefully concealed from nearly all, is over *one thousand.*

Sparty: That's quite a lot.

Condor: Hey, we're helping the local economies of 130-plus countries. It's not as if we need the money here. Plus, how else can Lockheed Martin, Boeing, Raytheon, Northrop Grumman, and General Dynamics continue to earn astronomical profits on overpriced weapons systems that rarely work?

Bo: Not to mention generously employ the big brass once they retire from serving us. Yes, sir-things couldn't be better in Bankrupt America, could they?

Sparty: Well, that does it for our maiden column in interview format. Condor will mercifully return next time with his regular pyrotechnics of prose.

−March 2009

---

* then Michigan Secretary of State Terri Lynn Land is now running for Carl Levin's seat in the U.S. Senate, and is the presumptive GOP nominee.

Dealers in Detroit

Fast forwarding four years, in this column Condor is again joined by his twin alter ego amigos. The Scene: America's bankrupt epicenter, Detroit, MI. The Time: Opening Day (Tigers-Yankees) April 5, 2013. All dialogue is based upon actual observation.

Condor: Four more years of MICMAC have merrily gone by...

Sparty: Whaddya mean "merrily"? There were no men in uniform inside the park gate entrances handing out free trinkets like last year, and no super cool jets flying overhead either. This silly sequester is starting to hurt me and my Pentagon pals in the advertising department.

Bo: And Chalmers Johnson has passed, so there is no one left who knows how many foreign bases we own. But in reviewing our previous column, just how were foreign economies helped, Condor?

Condor: Well, take South Korea. Our 28,000-plus troops stationed there enormously boost local businesses, like prostitution. We spend billions protecting the South Koreans, who have an economy only 40 times larger than their neighbors to the north.

Bo: Remember, our highest ranking Korean War POW stated our Air Forces carpet bombing destroyed nearly every major building in most of the North's cities and villages he saw.

Sparty: Always bringing up ancient history, Bo.

Condor: We just met a 30 year old high school graduate from affluent Oakland County who can't find work here but has taught English in South Korean schools the past three years. She actually *prefers* their not-as-quite profit driven way of life to ours!

Sparty: And the rad-libs say we only export high-tech weapons. We get rid of our commie-minded types (who else would leave the Land of the Free) and keep ourselves pure...USA! USA!

Condor: It was encouraging to see 140,000 metro Detroiters converge on Comerica-45,000 of whom were lucky enough to actually afford a ticket into the park.

Sparty: A $3-5 million boost to *our* local economy. How's that for a one-day surge, Mr. Bo?

Bo: Yes, $5 million is 1/36th of Verlander's new contract extension. Very distributionist.

Sparty: Well you can't say the Bengals aren't helping bring back the city. As is Kevin Orr, the new EM. He'll do for Detroit what he did for Chrysler.

Condor: Charge $700 an hour?

Sparty: Hey, Chrysler's out of bankruptcy and just had a great quarterly profits report. Even UAW prez Bob King is pleased with a third consecutive year of membership growth.

Bo: From 1.5 million members in '79...now back "up" to 382,000. Yes, cutting wages in half has stemmed the jobless tide...for now.

Sparty: Con, I still can't understand your lack of enthusiasm for our Big Five Defense Firms. These corporations represent American know-how and patriotic commitment to country we can all aspire to.

Condor: You neglected to add "unconscionable fleecing of taxpayers." When Lockheed merged with Martin Marietta, the company not only finagled $92million in golden parachutes for retiring execs, but actually got Uncle Sam to contribute over a third of the cost.

Bo: The Deepwater project to modernize the Coast Guard was awarded to Lockheed and Northrop Grumman in 2002 for $17 billion. Once hulls began cracking in the main ships being designed, making them unusable, Congress punished the firms by expanding the project and increasing the contract to $24 billion. The Feds did embarrass the two giants by taking away the management of the project from them, but presumably the added cash will cushion the blow.

Sparty: Nasty bureaucrats...but at least we helped out Boeing in its struggle with South Korea, right Con?

Condor: Correct, Spartamo. When South Korea was about to buy military aircraft from a French company that was better designed and $350 million cheaper than Boeing's F15K, the Pentagon intervened. They told our staunch East Asian allies we'd refuse to supply them with (Raytheon built) air-to-air missiles the jets use. That's how Boeing got its $4.46 billion contract with Seoul.

Bo: Plus, Boeing is one of 26 major corporations that paid *zero* federal income tax for the last four years-despite billions in profits.

Sparty: Isn't tax avoidance the essence of capitalism? You guys must admit it's perfectly legal...

Condor: True. Years of lobbying the first "C" in MICMAC, to create loopholes and reverse JFK's "bear any burden" rhetoric, have magnificently paid off. The Big Five are all chasing Bruce Jackson's Dream now.

Sparty: Bruce Jackson? I thought I knew everyone ESPN highlights. Who's he play for-the Supersonics?

Bo: Not a bad guess, Spartismo. Jackson is the quintessential MICMAC man. From Army Intelligence Officer, Bruce left the DoD to work for Lehman Brothers in its high leveraged heyday (before its self-destruction helped ferment the 2008 crash). He then spent a decade as Lockheed's VP for Strategy and Planning.

Condor: While at Lockheed he co-chaired Dole for President's Finance Committee, then led the 2000 GOP Platform Foreign Policy Subcommittee, largely enacted by Junior Bush. Now he runs the Project on Transitional Democracies, which advocates the Lockheed Martinization, er, integration of former Soviet satellites into Euro-Atlantic institutions.

Bo: Expanding NATO is Bruce's Big Concern. Though Senior Bush had pledged to Gorbachev we wouldn't push for this if Gorby peacefully pulled out his troops from Eastern Europe, the Clintons changed course. By coincidence, Lockheed made great inroads expanding its business into new NATO countries like Poland. Another win/win for MICMAC.

Sparty: Gee, why don't Judge Allen's fantasy football and baseball friends know any of this stuff?

Condor: Because Marx never saw an Opening Day, particularly one w/ prophylactic pre-game military salutes.

Bo: Sports, not religion, is the opium of the people.

Condor: More precisely, spectator sports is MICMAC'S opiate *for* the masses.

Sparty: Opening Day as Opium Den? Yeah, well...The Cats' 8-3 victory over the Soviet successor Evil Empire makes the "bearing of any (tax) burden" by the rest of us worth it. Go Tygers! Burn Bright in 2013...and Beyond.

−April 2013

Chapter Twelve

The Wills to Live

The fact that Garry Wills had, one month prior to the above mentioned ceremony, called for President Clinton's resignation for disgracing the Oval Office with the Lewinsky Scandal, epitomizes the Giant of the Pen's persona. Wills, in a journalistic career now spanning more than five decades, has spared no one in his relentless pursuit of Truth. The Northwestern professor's 75th birthday, commemorated today, seems reason enough to briefly contemplate his remarkable body of work.

Though referred to by the eminent John R. Allen, Jr. as "perhaps the most distinguished Catholic intellectual in America in the last 50 years," it is comical the responses Condor receives when mentioning Wills in conversation. They invariably fall into the 1) Who's Garry Wills? or 2) Oh, yes, I watch him Sunday mornings on ABC, categories. For the record, comparing Wills to rightwing commentator George Will (excepting the subject of baseball) is akin to comparing Babe Ruth to Babe Dahlgren.

Because you really can't compare Wills to anybody. The breath and depth of his tackled topics, from the American cinema to Shakespeare, from classical Greece and Rome to Machiavelli, from his shattering trilogy of New Testament works to the unflinching critiques of Catholic Church hierarchy, is astonishing. As an essayist alone, (chiefly as a 36 year regular for the *New York Review of Books)* his only rival on the American Experience is Gore Vidal.

Though he has written arguably the best books on Nixon (*Nixon Agonistes* landed him on Tricky Dick's master enemies list) and Reagan as well as the most trenchant essays on Carter and Clinton, Wills is perhaps most revered by scholars for his seminal dissections of our Nation's most sacred documents: Jefferson's Declaration of Independence (*Inventing America*), the Constitution (*Explaining America*), and the Gettysburg Address (*Lincoln at Gettysburg: The Words that Remade America*). But it is the early 19th century that I wish to highlight of Wills' fresh perspectives as yet to permeate conventional historical "wisdom."

"Negro President": Jefferson and the Slave Power makes the novel assertion (novel in the sense that all studies of Jefferson fail to mention, or at least give any emphasis to) that, but for slavery and the three-fifths clause of the Constitution, Jefferson could *not* have defeated President John Adams in the famous election of 1800. Though Jefferson won the electoral vote 73-65, Wills informs us that "slave voters" that year were between 12 and 16; votes "not based on the citizenry that could express its will but on the blacks owned by Southern masters." In terms of actual votes cast, "John Adams was reelected. The second revolution never occurred."

Not that Wills is unhappy with what resulted. He thinks Jefferson a greater president than either of Henry Adams' forbears. That Adams, our preeminent 19th century historian, wrote a nine volume tract on the administrations of Jefferson and James Madison has never prevented latter-day historians from misrepresenting his views on those presidencies. Scholars like Richard Hofstadter and Merrill Peterson adhere to the "family feud" thesis of history that Adams was defending his ancestors vs. the Jeffersonians.

Wills, in the brilliant *Henry Adams and the Making of America*, demonstrates that precisely the opposite happened. Henry Adams thought that the Jeffersonians *created* a national unity necessary for the young republic to flourish. By reviewing all nine volumes, and not cherry-picking a few chapters, Wills makes the case that Jefferson's decentralizing ideology failed to materialize during his time in power. And that it *couldn't have*, lest the "projection of American power abroad (and) an energetic adoption of the means of western expansion" would never have occurred. Wills believes, as did Henry Adams, that these were good things.

A third major Wills enlightenment for history students concerns Alexis de Tocqueville's *Democracy in America*. Wills, in "Did Tocqueville 'Get' America" (*NYRB* April 29, 2004) challenges the standard conservative assertion that his is "the best book on democracy, and best book written on America," (Harvey Mansfield). Wills states, "Some people are astonished that a 26 year old Frenchman with imperfect English could write the best book on America, after a brief visit to the country. I am astonished that anyone can think that he did."

In a 3000 word analysis, Wills proceeds to demonstrate how little Tocqueville actually saw of America in his famous trip of 1831-32. The Frenchman never attended a town hall meeting, never saw an American university, never mentions any academics or artists, and that "most of his opinions were formed at his first encounter with an idea."

A former Jesuit seminarian, Wills dedicated one of his nearly 40 books to his mentor Father Joseph Fisher, whom he called "the sanest guide." In an all too often insane world, Garry Wills has been, for Condor at least, the sanest guide imaginable. Seventy-five years hence, John Allen's description of the American Augustine may turn out to be but muted understatement.

—May 22, 2009

3M Nation

On December 12, 2012, at Sandy Hook Elementary School in Newtown, Connecticut, 20 year old Adam Lanza used his mother's constitutionally protected (via a 2008 U.S. Supreme Court decision) .223 Bushmaster XM 15-E2S rifle, complete with multiple 30 round magazines, to kill, by firing 154 bullets in less than five minutes, 20 children and six adults. Immediately prior to the rampage, Lanza had shot and killed his mother, a known gun enthusiast, at their nearby home. Immediately after the carnage, he fired a 155th bullet, killing himself.

It was the eighth "mass murder" (the FBI defines this term as killing four or more persons at a particular event with no cooling-off period) in the U.S. in 2012. According to the University of Chicago Crime Lab, 87 gun deaths occur, on average, each day across the land. The gun Lanza used was manufactured by Freedom Works, a corporation owned by private equity giant Cerberus Capital Management. Cerberus happens to be the 11th largest U.S. federal contractor, with taxpayer-gifted revenue alone totaling $4.8 billion in 2010. It decided, because of poor publicity its weapon was receiving post-Newtown massacre, to sell Freedom Works on December 18.

It took, per usual, the inimitable Garry Wills to provide *lux et veritas* ("light and truth," motto of his alma mater Yale) on this latest horror. In a *New York Review of Books* blog posted three days after the killings entitled "Our Moloch," Wills wrote that the ancient and demonic god of child sacrifice referenced in the Old Testament, the "sign of a deeply degraded culture," has been revived by our societal gun reverence. He pointed out that fealty to our Moloch—The Gun:

1. "destroys the reasoning process…we are required to deny that there is any connection between the fact that we have the greatest number of guns in private hands and the greatest number of deaths from them."
2. has the power to turn "all our politicians as a class into invertebrate and mute attendants at the shrine."
3. distorts constitutional thinking. Enslavement to Moloch "says the 'right to bear arms,' a military term, gives anyone anywhere…the power to mow down civilians with military weapons."

But gun worshippers were only momentarily muted by the angry voices of Wills and other blasphemers. Less than four months later the *Wall Street Journal* posted the dystopian headline "Pro-Gun Laws Gain Ground," (April 4, 2013). In fully half of the country's state legislatures, bills had been sent to governors to *weaken* gun-control laws, making one wonder what will happen to the other 25 states after the next Newtown.

Of course, the god Gun is not the sole deity sacred in American culture. Mammon, the New Testament pejoratively named god of material wealth and greed, is corporate personhood's fixation without peer, the sine qua non of capitalism. The sole purpose of all corporations (the persons that matter to our government) is to make as much profit as possible, so Cerberus and all gun manufacturers benefit handsomely from having sold an estimated 310 million civilian guns in America today (about one per non-corporate person). To interfere with these earnings is to upend the free market system itself, an obviously abhorrent thought to those in power.

Naturally, in a county where 75% of citizens profess a faith in Trinitarian Christianity, a third deity is needed as well. (It is useful to remember that Trinity was the code name for the first atomic bomb successfully detonated-by the U.S. Army three weeks before Hiroshima-in New Mexico July 1945. Thus was an American stamp placed on the seemingly endless musings of the fourth century philosopher Saint Augustine.) Condor proposes a feminine spirit embodying a limitless combination of celebrity and sex   appeal, with iconic Hollywood star Marilyn Monroe as proffered idol. In a recent poll Monroe, more than a half-century after her death, was accorded the title "No. 1 Sex Symbol of All-Time"-the figure women want to emulate and men simply want. Her troubled life and tragic suicide, despite seemingly "having it all," corresponds neatly with the road current U.S. political non-thought is racing down.

Moloch, Mammon, Monroe…a 3M nation of Old, New, and American Testaments that a majority believe is Christian at its core, but whose actions are best expressed in the Chesterton quote above. Our epidemic of violence reflects our rage at having our desires unfulfilled, desires that we, unaware, borrow from others, especially in the modern age of ubiquitous advertising, because we ourselves know not what to desire.

An insatiable appetite for celebrity gossip/spectator sports updates is fed round-the-clock by MICMAC media, effectively turning attention away from unfortunate facts like an income equality system that ranks last among 22 "developed" nations from Japan, Canada, Australia, New Zealand, and 18 in Europe. Looking at the gun homicide rate among these same countries, the U.S. average is 15 times that of the others. The 310 million firearms estimate in our land excludes our military's ownership of most of the planet's weapons of mass destruction. If the exegetes who argue Christ is Peace are right, the United States has travelled a considerably distance in demonstrating it is the most unchristian nation around.

−April 2013

Time for a
Third Way?

On June 26th the U.S. House of Representatives debated and voted on a monumental bill concerning carbon emission reduction, which GOP leader and bill opponent John Boehner labeled, "the most historic legislation of the past hundred years." Not knowing the bill's fate, which had narrowly passed (219-212) upon largely party lines, Condor, en route to dinner, turned on, at 6:30 p.m., the CBS radio news. The lead story was continued coverage of the death, from more than 24 hours before, of a bizarre American recording artist. The second story mentioned the climate bill, but only to say that the House, while debating it, took a moment of silence to honor the bizarre American recording artist. No further information about the proposed legislation was forthcoming.

It is difficult to overstate the precariousness of our current situation. We are, in the wake of last year's spectacular collapse of the financial system, in "therapy phase," says Harvard history professor Niall Ferguson. The Therapy we are using is two-fold: 1) a massive injection of liquidity from the Federal Reserve into our largest banks, and 2) the most enormous fiscal stimulus (debt) package since World War II. Ferguson thinks the two procedures cannot be simultaneously successfully used. If he's right, a long term worldwide depression is just around the corner.

Unfortunately, the likelihood of this depression is not the worst of our problems. The scientific news on global warming, as opposed to propaganda still given shrift by such Paleolithic publications as the *Wall Street Journal*, gets more urgent by the minute. In just the two years since the Intergovernmental Panel on Climate Change issued its last (dire) report, leading climatologists now believe the pace of global warming has become *even more rapid*. The Guru Himself, NASA's Dr. James Hansen, says that 350 carbon parts per million (ppm) is the goal we need for atmospheric levels-it was previously thought that 450-550 was a level that could have kept, though with moderate disruption, civilization somewhat close to what we've known.

The trouble is that we're at 387 ppm now-it was 275 ppm before the Industrial Revolution. So President Obama's bill, and the multi-national December meeting in Copenhagen for worldwide carbon reduction, as ground-breaking as they promise to be, may still be too little, too late.

Henry Adams, for the Michael Jackson Generation, was a renowned 19th century writer and historian. The "confession" he penned which introduced this piece (and confession it was, for Adams was scion of the most distinguished family in American political history) was written in 1910. That same year, perhaps not coincidentally, saw the publication of G.K. Chesterton's *What's Wrong with the World*, which led to Chesterton's introduction of Distributism, a Third Way (between capitalism and socialism) economic philosophy.

Inspired by Pope Leo XIII's two-decades-old encyclical *Rerum Novarum* (Of New Things) which formulated a dynamic set of economic principles -the first being that the remuneration of labor "cannot be left to the mechanical play of market forces" -Chesterton demolished what free-marketers have championed for the last century with the words "Too much capitalism does not mean too many capitalists, but too few capitalists." Today, the "too few" have asked for, and received, gargantuan government bailouts, leaving the rest of society in the lurch. The prospect of *inverted totalitarianism*, a term coined by political philosopher Sheldon Wolin to describe how our corporations are becoming the effective equivalents of Hitler and Stalin, seems increasingly inevitable.

Fortunately, there is Chesterton's Third Way to consider. Distributism envisions, first and foremost, the protection of private property.

Ownership of the means of production "should be spread as widely as possible among the general populace." Distributism favors local production regarding items like food and clothing, rather than mass-producers and foreign reliance. The proposal to farm large tracts of vacant Detroit land could be one such promising example.

Distributism also envisions elimination of the current for-profit banking system, something which may upon reflection appear obvious to all but those in the behemoth financial institutions that have so greatly damaged the world's economy. Credit unions, noticeably unscathed during the recent meltdown, would receive more favorable governmental treatment.

Nothing exemplifies the absurdity of our current predicament better than last week's news of auto supplier Visteon's bankruptcy. In its court petition, the company asks that $31 million of retiree health care and life insurance benefits, negotiated and earned by nearly 4500 retired workers, be completely eliminated. In a separate motion, the company seeks permission for $30.1 million in funding for bonuses for its top 100 executives, those remarkable performers who have brought about the bankruptcy in the first place. This neatly proposed theft echoes Henry Adams with but one proviso-the laborers, in our age of Instant Information, are not likely to remain "consenting parties" much longer.

-June 2009

Too Big to Fail, Too Big to Jail

In the first 13 years of the 20th century, New York Giants pitcher Christy "Big Six" Mathewson dominated big league hitters as no one had before him. At his peak in 1908, Matty won 37 games and had a career best .374 Park Adjusted Pitching Average (PAPA).* Idol to millions, he is often called America's first genuine sports hero.

In the first 13 years of the 21st century, New York (and thus big league finance) was also ruled by a Big Six. Exactly 100 seasons after Mathewson's peak, this Big Six's dominance led the country to near-economic collapse, while sending shock waves that reached all the world's financial capitals. Banks JP Morgan Chase, Bank of America, Citigroup, Wells Fargo, Goldman Sachs, and Morgan Stanley, idols to millions of get-rich-quick investors, had grown from having assets worth 17% of U.S. GDP in 1995 to 63% by 2008. If most Americans were unaware of this astonishing growth, they might have at least noticed that the number of sports' stadiums and arenas that have bank names went from zero in 1997 to 20 a mere thirteen years later. Baseball's latest is Citigroup's Citifield, heir to Mathewson's Polo Grounds, where the New York Mets now play.

The deregulation of the late 1990s and the tripling of lending leverage led to the near collapse. On September 18, 2008 Federal Reserve Chairman Benny Bernanke told an assembled group of congressional leaders that "if we don't act in a very huge way, you can expect another Great Depression, and this is going to be worse." The Fed then provided $16 trillion in liquidity to supplement the $700 billion direct bailout aid approved by a frightened Congress.

These moves saved the banks, as all now know, at a tremendous cost to nearly everyone else. In response, Congress passed the

Dodd-Frank Wall Street Reform and Consumer Protection Act, whose three main purposes are "to promote the financial stability of the U.S. by improving accountability and transparency in the financial system, to end "too big to fail," and to "promote the American taxpayer by ending bailouts." The legislation was passed, and signed by President Barack Obama, in July 2010.

Does the legislation provide significant reform? Regarding "improving accountability and transparency," consider the enormous covert derivatives trading the Big Six now do. Over-the-counter (OTC) "interest rate swaps" totaled $176 *trillion* for the six month period ending December 31, 2010. Six months later, with Dodd-Frank

These contracts have zero transparency and zero regulation.

in effect, the number grew to $190 trillion. These contracts have zero transparency and zero regulation. Knowledgeable specialists conclude that only the U.S. Treasury itself is the partner for most if not all of Morgan Stanley's swaps, which increased its derivatives portfolio by a mind-boggling $8 trillion in a six-month period.

The Securities Exchange Act of 1934, still in effect, has a little known provision that states when the U.S. national security is at risk, the Executive Branch may exempt companies from ordinary legal obligations like keeping accurate "books, records, and accounts" in accordance with "generally accepted accounting principles." This authority was delegated (reportedly for the first time) in May 2006 by then-President Bush to National Intelligence Director John Negroponte. There is nothing to suggest Obama has revoked that edict. In other words, the Big Six could be completely hiding the nature of their true financial health, lest the house of cards collapses and panic ensues.

To end "too big to fail" is Dodd-Frank's second stated goal. Today, the Big Six are bigger than ever, avoid paying U.S. taxes like never before, and have the aforementioned derivatives in larger sums than during 2008. Simon Johnson's *13 Bankers* eloquently makes the case to simply break up the largest banks. He sums up the three major problems with them: 1) when they're about to fail, they must be bailed out, 2) this gives the Big Six an *institutionalized* incentive to take excessive risk-since they know they'll be bailed out, and 3) they have an inherently unfair advantage over smaller banks and lending entities. If everyone knows a bailout is the implicit backup, bond investors will lend money at lesser rates to the big boys.

In 2009, there was a $34 billion subsidy, in effect, for the 18 largest U.S. banks. Three years later, the subsidy grew to $64 billion for just the *five* largest. This hardly constitutes reform.

"To protect consumers from abusive financial services practices," is the fourth stated Dodd-Frank goal. On March 6, 2013, U.S. Attorney General Eric Holder, testifying before a Senate committee, said that prosecuting giant banks for potential crimes "will have a negative effect on the national economy, perhaps even the world economy." It is therefore best left undone.

The Big Six leadership thus knows that not only has no one been prosecuted for the previous heists, no one is likely to be fingered in the future, either. If this isn't cause enough to break up the biggest banks, ala Teddy Roosevelt and the Standard Oil Trust, Condor is lost to suggest what could be. Unfortunately, it's going to take the next crisis, looming over a not-too-distant horizon, and certain to be worse than the last, before Washington gets around to recognizing, let alone doing anything about, the patently obvious.

-May 2013

---

*   For an explanation of the PAPA formula, see the author's *How Could You Trade Billy Pierce?*, p.16-17.

Chapter Fourteen

You're Gonna Cry...96 Years

Ben "Bugsy" Bernanke wants to expand the Federal Reserve Board's already virtually limitless powers by making consumer protection a new "central part" of that body's role. The Fed's mandated goals are achieving full employment and price stability-the proposed protection (racket) should give all pause. Fed Chairman Ben testified last week before a finally skeptical Congress that belatedly hopes to reign in the secretive board after nearly a century of "We Can't Tell You What We Know, But Trust Us, Anyway"-style governance of monetary policy.

A bit of history is in order. Following the panic of 1907, a financial crisis of no small magnitude, bankers and their conservative allies pushed for a central banking system that would be entirely privately owned -i.e., no government interference. They wanted geographically spread branches able to issue currency during periodic money shortages.

Opponents, mainly western and southern populists and some progressives, feared the eastern "Money Trust" and wanted a government controlling authority. Their champion was thrice-defeated presidential nominee William Jennings Bryan, deliverer of the famous "Cross of Gold" speech, who eventually resigned as Secretary of State in a futile attempt to keep the U.S. out of World War I. A Wall Street bagman labeled the proposed government intervention "the slime of Bryanism."

Compromise came under newly elected (in 1912) President Woodrow Wilson. Twelve regional banks, from Boston to San Francisco, would operate privately, yet all were to be placed under a supervisory body-the Federal Reserve Board. The Act passed both houses of Congress and was signed by Wilson on the fateful day of December 23, 1913. (Few noticed that Congress had just ceded its authority to "coin money" under Article 1, Sec. 8 of the Constitution to a new, quasi-public institution.)

Bryan had fought heroically for government control, but his biographer notes he "apparently gave little thought to the possibility that the Board might become the servant of the bankers." In short, Bryan trusted Wilson, who was to make the first appointments. Wilson, who knew little of banking but much of who had bankrolled his election, stacked the Board with bank and Chamber of Commerce presidents; for diversity he picked a railroad tycoon. Progressives were outraged, but the die had been cast.

Ninety-six years and two Depressions later, much ridiculed (by the Establishment) U.S. Rep. Ron Paul of Texas has written a bill that would submit the Fed to an audit of what it actually does. Surprisingly, more than half of his colleagues have stumbled on as co-sponsors. Bernanke, of course, vehemently opposes the bill.

> **Ron Paul of Texas has written a bill that would submit the Fed to an audit of what it actually does.**

The Secrets of the Temple, as William Greider titled his 1987 classic account of the Fed's inner workings, *must ever so remain.*

Perhaps taking a cue from the Fed don, this month Bush the Younger Torture Memo Father and warrantless wiretap guru John "Blank" Yoo defended his Constitution-shredding days at the Department of Justice with a *Wall Street Journal* op-ed (July 16). Yoo wrote "It was instantly clear after 9/11 that our security agencies knew little about Al Qaeda's inner workings (and) could not predict where it might strike next." Excepting the CIA report Bush received 36 days before 9/11 entitled "Bin Laden Determined to Strike Inside U.S.," only the (coincidentally) 36th time Al Qaeda and/or Bin Laden had been mentioned in a Bush Presidential Daily

Briefing, including specific references to New York City federal buildings, Yoo is probably correct.

Yoo was the attorney who gave Bush the novel concept that the executive branch need not involve its legislative counterpart to start wars, except *ceremonially*. The Pride of the Federalist Society also promotes a version of the Unitary Executive Theory that makes presidents subject to no law during time of war. These ideas, says University of Chicago law professor Cass Sunstein, leaves Yoo at odds with, among others, "James Madison, Thomas Jefferson, Alexander Hamilton, John Adams, and George Washington." Let his supporters not so Swiftly believe that the Founding Houyhnhnms could have been all wrong, though, and their Y(ah)oo right.

Usurping the Constitution then, a favorite pastime of those in power, continues in almost unabated fashion. So may your next Depression-induced vodka-flavored drink include three limes for the "slime of Bryanism." That's to honor each electoral effort of the venturesome Volcano who vociferated valiantly but very vainly for the voiceless vassals, the once and future We the People.

-July 2009

Blowhards on Blowback

> *"For every action, there is an equal and opposite reaction."*
>
> *–Newton's Third Law of Motion*

The term "blowback" was coined by the Central Intelligence Agency in its "after-action" report of its role in toppling democratically elected Iranian president Mohammad Mossadegh in August 1953. To protect British oil interests in that Middle East nation, the U.S. installed the brutally repressive Shah-who in turn was driven from power in 1979. When President Jimmy Carter, against U.S. State Department advice, allowed the Shah's entry into the U.S. for medical treatment, Iranian students and militants promptly took hostage 66 Americans from the U.S. Embassy in Iran; 52 were held for 444 days. The Iranian Hostage Crisis immobilized the Carter presidency and practically gifted the nation Ronald "Bedtime for Bonzo" Reagan.

Blowback, then, refers specifically to covert action taken by our government around the world without its citizens knowing what is being done. Chalmers Johnson, former CIA consultant turned author, wrote three books known as "The Blowback Trilogy," the first of which (actually called *Blowback)* was published the year prior to the 9/11 attacks. Through Johnson's lens, many examples were provided of terrorist actions taken in response to U.S. imperialism-the most horrific, of course, being the Al Qaeda attacks of 9/11.

Nine days after those attacks, which claimed the lives of nearly 3000 people, President George W. Bush, obviously without having read *Blowback*, and arguably without ever having read anything at all, stated, "Americans are asking, 'why do they hate us?' They hate what they see right here in this chamber: a democratically elected government…They hate our freedoms: our freedom of religion, our freedom of speech, our freedom to vote and assemble and disagree with each other."

Stirring rhetoric it was, except that admitted terrorist mastermind Osama bin Laden told the world the reasons why he attacked us. He cited 1) our troop presence on Saudi Arabian "sacred" (to Islam) soil, 2) U.S. imposed sanctions on Iraq, which reportedly took the lives of 500,000 Iraqi children, and 3) U.S. complicity in Israel's decades-long occupation and mistreatment of Palestinians.

Fast forward twelve years. The Boston Marathon Bombings, two weeks past as I pen these words, killed three and injured a reported 282 people. Coverage of this event has been, as all non-comatose individuals are aware, virtually 24/7 in MICMAC media for the fortnight.

Nine days after these attacks, Vice President Joe Biden, at a memorial service for the officer slain by the bombing suspects, said that the terrorists who perpetrated the attacks hated the U.S. "for our open society, our system of justice that guarantees freedom, and the access of every American to opportunity. It infuriates them."

Again, the surviving suspect has reportedly told interrogators a somewhat different story-saying that he and his brother were motivated by the U.S. invasions of Iraq and Afghanistan. The *New York Times* actually reported this tiny bit of information, but predictably buried it in paragraph 24 of its story "Boston Suspects Are Seen as Self-Taught and Fueled by Web." The innocuous language:

"The ex-brother-in-law of the suspect said, 'he had been *enamored* of *conspiracy theories,* and that he was *concerned* by the wars in the Middle East.'" (Emphasis mine).

Note the subtlety. *The Times* won't ignore the obvious-that might make people question its accuracy. By downplaying it, though, *The Times* says "See, we reported all there is to know, and we'll decide what angle to give the public." The story headline says it all.

MICMAC media, interestingly, had nary a mention of the 29 bombings that killed 75 and wounded 356 the same day as the Boston tragedy. That was because these hundreds of victims were in Iraq. The 24 killed in bombings three days before received no mention, either, nor did the 32 killed in Bagdad four days later with 65 more wounded at a pool hall in a mall. Nor, of course, did the fact that suicide bombings were virtually nonexistent before March 2003 (the month the U.S. invaded), and have become so routine as to no longer qualify as news (except perhaps to the victims' loved ones.)

Unofficial MICMAC mouthpiece Tom Brokaw stated on the day of the Boston bombings, "everyone has to understand tonight, however, beginning tomorrow morning early there's going to be much tougher security considerations across the country. However exhausted we may be by then, we have to live with them and get along and go forward and not let them bring us to our knees."

In other words, regarding the reduction in civil liberties we've "enjoyed" since 9/11-*You Ain't Seen Nothin' Yet.*

Why on earth anyone would attempt to make a connection between a terrorist act and the terrorist's stated reasons for committing it is beyond Condor's intellect. It is much easier to believe the Bush and Biden logic, and accept the Brokaw preparatory pronouncement. That way we can both perpetrate an unending cycle of violence destined to get worse, and tighten the noose around the neck of our steadily eroding civil liberties. It's a MICMAC twofer.

---

* One spectacular, though completely forgotten, example of blowback occurred on March 1, 1954 at the U.S.Capitol. Five members of

Congress were shot and wounded by four Puerto Rican nationalists who were eventually tried, convicted, and sentenced in U.S. courts to virtual lifetime terms. One of the nationalists said, "I came not to kill anyone, but to die for Puerto Rico." Since we had ruled that island since 1898, and appointed governors who often took Puerto Rican money and doled it out to U.S. corporate interests via no-bid contracts while the overwhelming majority of the population remained impoverished, one might envision a few natives getting upset.

—May 2013

Chapter Fifteen

Malaise and the Mother Lode

The current health care "debate" combined with the recent death of Senator Edward Kennedy reminds Condor of a time not so long ago in a land not quite far away-America 1979. Then President Jimmy Carter, having pledged to provide national health insurance in his winning election of 1976, had failed by the Summer of '79 to articulate a set of principles for NHI, much less propose concrete legislation. The reason he gave was cost. "We can't afford to do everything." Carter said at the time. His advisors agreed.

But Kennedy, with considerable support from the (then) powerful United Auto Workers, had made national health insurance his top legislative priority. In fact, Carter's "reneging" on this issue may have been the primary reason the Massachusetts Democrat would make his only, and as it turned out unsuccessful, challenge for a White House that had once been seemingly his for the asking. "We've got to control costs," Kennedy told Newsweek "(Health care) will go to 9% of gross domestic product next year."

How quaint. Fast forward thirty years. Healthcare costs are now 17% of GDP, steadily rising, and far in excess of any other western country's. What has happened and why?

The U.S. Supreme Court decided in *Goldfarb v Virginia* (1975) that lawyers, and by extension physicians, are engaged in interstate commerce and thus subject to antitrust regulation. This ruling caused the American Medical Association to change its ethical guidelines to state that practicing medicine was both a profession *and* a business, opening the doors to physician/pharmaceutical partnerships that have since been a financial boon to both.

Three major developments have emerged since that time, according to former *New England Journal of Medicine* Editor-in-Chief Arnold Relman. First, the U.S., as compared to other nations, has grown an abundance of specialists vis-à-vis primary care doctors. These specialists are on average much more highly paid than other physicians.

Second, there is no financial incentive for physicians, hospitals and clinics *not* to use expensive technology (available in other countries but not used nearly as much). They are all reimbursed by their insurer for most of what they collectively charge patients.

Third, our hospitals and clinics, to a much greater extent than just a generation ago, are *investor* owned, and that means one thing: profit, not health care, is the driving force behind these institutions. And to compete with them, the non-profit

> ...profit, not health care, is the driving force behind these institutions.

hospitals feel they must promote themselves, which explains the explosion in recent years of (cost-added) advertisements telling us why "X, Y, or Z Hospital" is the only place to go to have your goiter removed or kidney stones crushed.

To Relman's three developments Condor adds a fourth "problem." Problem is euphemistically placed in quotes because it is, in fact the Mother Lode of all fiscal nightmares. Medicare, the government-run medical benefits program which covers 43 million Americans aged 65 and older, has been running a structural deficit since it was instituted in 1965. It is a "pay as you go" system; currently 3.9 workers' contributions (in taxes) are used to pay for each recipient's benefits. By 2030 it will be 2.4 workers, so taxes will have to be increased, or benefits cut, to maintain the current stream of revenue.

But the real nightmare is what economists call the "infinite horizon discounted value" i.e., the amount needed today to cover all unfunded liabilities of what has been promised recipients but has no funding mechanism in place. This figure, according to Dallas Federal Reserve Board CEO Richard Fisher, is an astounding $85.6 trillion. That comes to $330,000 for *each* man, woman and child in America.

Why are these factors so unknown to the general public? Well, our government continually makes easily refutable claims-we're "winning" in Iraq, occupying Afghanistan for the next thousand years makes us safer, bailing out insipidly run banks will avoid bigger financial meltdowns. It is little wonder, then, that the current health care discussion has been effectively cast in terms of guaranteed non-reform. Washington courtiers Disney, Viacom, General Electric, Time Warner, and Rupert the Fox frame the debate between the GOP-favored status quo and variations of Obamacare, but none of them address the looming insolvency issue, or the others mentioned here.

The time is moving inexorably closer to the Storm of Storms. Perhaps our Pentagon masters, erstwhile recipients of $100 billion of real money graciously gifted by Ronald Reagan to build his fictional Strategic Defense Initiative Missile Shield (which Ted Kennedy immediately and ungraciously dubbed "Star Wars") can, from the remarkable research completed in that ill-fated but noble program, make sturdy Umbrella Shields for us all. In the meantime, resonant with the information shared today, may we wistfully pine...for the Malaise Days of '79.

−August 2009

Vioxx con Dios

Malaise was one emotion not felt by the management of Merck & Co. in 1979. In June of that year, Merck was awarded entrance into the ultimate club of capitalism-the Dow Jones Component 30. Not only was it the first pharmaceutical to make the Big 30 (Johnson & Johnson and Pfizer would follow, respectively, two and three decades later), it had been growing at an annualized rate of 13.1% since its merger with Sharpe & Dohme in 1953.

Twenty years later (1999) Merck introduced the anti-arthritis drug Vioxx to the market. It was FDA-approved despite studies that indicated an enormously increased risk of heart attack by users. These findings Merck worked to suppress, and it was later learned that four of six FDA advisory panel members had financial ties to the company.

By 2004, the popular drug (20 million users and $2.5 billion in annual sales, thanks to heavy media promotion featuring ice skating icon Dorothy Hamill) had to be withdrawn. It had caused between 26,000 and 55,000 fatal heart attacks. Merck in 2007 settled 27,000 civil suits for $4.5 billion, the largest such payout ever. Eventually Merck pled guilty to criminal charges for its Vioxx marketing, costing an additional $950 million. However, company executives were quite relieved, since Wall Street analysts had originally speculated that the total costs of the Vioxx fiasco would run from between $10 to $25 billion.

Fellow Dow Jones luminaries Pfizer and Johnson & Johnson would follow, respectively, three and five years later with criminal actions settled, too. In 2010, Pfizer was fined $2.3 billion for marketing a drug in ways never proven safe or effective, breaking Eli Lilly's $1.4 billion record fine for the same crime the year before.

In 2012, Johnson & Johnson was clipped $1.2 billion for 238,000 violations of Medicare fraud laws. That same year, Abbott was fined $1.5 billion for effectively doing what Pfizer and Eli Lilly did (no one has claimed that this is a particularly creative outlaw industry).

Also in 2012, Amgen settled for $762 million for misbranding a drug. This came on the heels of Bristol Meyers Squib's $515 million government settlement for its off-label marketing, pricing fraud, and kickback scheme.

The seven companies mentioned above are, perhaps not quite so coincidentally, the seven largest Fortune 500 pharmaceuticals based in the U.S. In the spirit of fairness, Condor does not claim that U.S. corporations have a monopoly on criminal activity. London-based GlaxoSmithKline (fourth largest pharmaceutical in the world) was hit in 2012 with a $3 billion fine in the largest health care fraud case in history, perhaps to show the colonials their mother country should not be taken for granted.

Such roguish behavior can't go unrewarded, so when the time came in 2009 for President Barack Obama to reform our byzantine health care system, all of Big Pharma was included for discussions at the table. Along with for-profit hospital representatives and health insurance executives, Big Pharma made sure that any "reform" would benefit their respective industries. Obama and leading Democrats nicely cooperated.

The initial issue was destroying, at the outset, any hope for a single payer system ("Medicare for all"). In a brilliant tactical maneuver that MICMAC media declined to highlight, Montana Senator Max Baucus, chair of the committee charged with opening the health care reform debate, made sure that zero of the 28 expert witnesses called to testify were single payer proponents. Polls at the time indicated a majority of both physicians and the general public favored this type of system, but Baucus had received hundreds of thousands of dollars in campaign donations from the health industries.

Progressives then fell back to proposing a single payer *option*, merely to compete with private health care and not even taxpayer-subsidized. But competition is the last thing the health care industry wants. It would cut into the companies' breathtakingly large profits. The Act, popularly known as Obamacare, was passed, without the single payer (or public) option, in March 2010.

It was by then known, though hardly reported, that the Obama Administration and the health industries had cut two secret deals. The first was that the single payer option, despite being rhetorically supported by the President, would not be part of the final bill. In exchange the health industries agreed to support the bill.

> **...the Obama Administration and the health industries had cut two secret deals.**

The second secret deal concerned Big Pharma. The White House agreed not to use its leverage with Congress to bargain for lower drug prices. It also agreed to not shift some drugs for Medicare Part B to Part D, which would have reduced industry profits. In exchange, Big Pharma agreed to cut costs by $80 billion over 10 years. Since their projected sales promptly sky rocketed $137 billion over four years, this was quite a worthwhile trade.

The secret deals are totally consistent with the lack of transparency the Obamaites have exhibited on other issues throughout their tenure. As for the people who prematurely went to see their (nondrug) Maker, they can rest peacefully knowing the settlements paid out by Big Pharma to their loved ones are but a fiscally prudent alternative (Pfizer, Johnson & Johnson, and Merck had combined 2012 profits of $26 billion) to operating corporations with an iota of integrity. The Malaise Days of '79 continue to improve with age as we watch our present system's delusional degeneration.

-June 2013

Chapter Sixteen

General Impressions

Witness the end of the Empire – The Romans of our time.

–Sam Roberts

The most recent Pew poll indicates that Americans support the proposed "surge" in Afghanistan by an impressive 57-35% margin. Not only does a majority of citizens approve of President Obama's action to contain about 100 Al-Qaeda members, they should be greatly heartened by the knowledge that said surge is already working. It is a success for the following groups and persons:

Private Contractors. Though rarely mentioned in the mainstream media, there are now about 105,000 PCs in Afghanland, or roughly one per projected U.S. soldier. That figure is up to a whopping 40% since June. Seventy-eight thousand are locals, but international corporations led by Dyncorp (proven wasters of millions of dollars in Iraq) are employing the natives at competitive rates.

Base builders. The virtually unnoticed "embassy" being constructed in Islamabad, which will soon serve as diplomatic center for Af-Pak (at the "cost-efficient" price of $736 million), is to be the second largest such structure on the planet. Only our fortress in Baghdad's Green Zone will contain more fast-food restaurants. These embassies, of course, are/will be walled-in compounds and city-states within nations, but should impress as tourist attractions. Afghan's $200 million Bagram Air Base, left by the Soviets as a reminder of *their* success, leads dozens of smaller but significant outposts now underway throughout the provinces.

The Afghan government. The Karzai regime, ranked among the five most corrupt in the world, will now get many billions for "development." Thirteen billion dollars already spent in this area has admittedly gone to waste, but after only eight years there it is reasonable to assume we've ironed out the kinks. Karzai's brother, a major drug lord, is on the CIA payroll, so one can't claim that the drug trade at least isn't being developed. And now the Afghan Prez says his forces won't be ready to be on their own "for 15 or 20 years," so the U.S. taxpayer can look forward to being the gifter who keeps on giving.

The trainees. One quarter of these Afghan stalwarts deserted last year, and one third of those completing training are only attending 50% of the required courses. But when these ill-equipped and drug-addicted protectors reach the desired number of 400,000, Lanctotians should sleep more easily at night.*

The Taliban. Our own officials in Kabul admit that western intelligence agencies within NATO are bribing our enemies so that supply convoys can reach intended destinations. Also, many private contractors are reportedly paying a cut (10% to 20%) to the insurgents on most contracts. It is not true, though, that the State Department has proposed putting the Treasury Department on the terror-watch list.

The NSA/CIA. A threefold surge in diplomatic, intelligence, and civilian officials is expected. The CIA, now demoted to fourth place in our extra-constitutional intelligence agency hierarchy, can perhaps break into the top three again. Our super secret National Security Agency (number of employees -classified) is now building, for $2 billion, a data info center in Utah that will not only be much larger than the U.S. Capital, but will use as much energy as every house in Salt Lake City combined. More Afghan money means more for the NSA, too. We must continue to care and feed Big Brother.

Centcom. During the Vietnam War, the power that Military Assistance Command-Vietnam (MACV) had on overall military strategy was limited. There were three other regional commands, and there was a Cold War going on. Today, U.S. Central Command covers 20 Middle East and Central Asian countries, covering all key ones in the "War on Terror," and dominates U.S. foreign policy as no other single organization in our nation's annals. Scott Ritter argues Centcom "has morphed into a virtual nation-state, operating largely independent of traditional checks and balances." The charismatic General David Petreaus runs this entity.

Stanley McCrystal. General McC, whose adroitness in covering up the truth of NFL star Pat Tillman's death by friendly fire earned him not punishment but promotion, is now being lionized by a fawning media ever ready to make new heroes. Can David P. or Stan the Man join the Pantheon of history book generals like Pershing, MacArthur, Patton, and Schwarzkopf? Stay tuned.

One general ignored by our high school texts is Smedley Butler. Up until World War II, Old Gimlet Eye was the most decorated Marine in U.S. history. But he's been left out of the Pantheon for good reason. Of his 33 year career in the Corps he stated,

"I spent most of my time as a high class muscle man for Big Business, for Wall Street and the bankers. In short, I was a racketeer, a gangster for capitalism. I helped make Mexico safe for American oil interests in 1914. I helped make Haiti and Cuba a decent place for the National City Bank boys to collect revenues in. I helped purify Nicaragua for Brown Brothers Banking House in 1902-1912." Butler also mentioned success in Honduras, the Dominican Republic, and China, before concluding,

"Looking back on it, I might have given Al Capone a few hints. The best he could do was operate his racket in three districts. I operated on three continents."

Today, our military operates on *six* continents. How long a nation nearing bankruptcy continues to allow these workings will be fascinating fodder for future historians.

-September 2009

---

* So named for zealous and able Detroit area attorney Todd Lanctot, enthusiast (with many others) of the "We're Fighting Them There so We Don't Have to Fight Them Here" doctrine.

The Dirty Dozen

"Being called a traitor by Dick Cheney is the highest honor you can give an American."

−Edward Snowden

The Great Transformation, in just less than twelve years, of the United States from democratic leader of the free world to its laughingstock is nearly complete. June 5th's bombshell of Verizon's blanket release of millions of customers' phone records to be combed over by the National Security Agency, an unconstitutional exercise of naked power was, by June 6th, the less spectacular of the two totalitarian touchdowns by an out-of-control federal apparatus whose roguish spokespeople now unmistakably merely masquerade as representatives of a free people.

The Day Before D-Day revelation, in a scoop by reporter and longtime civil liberties stalwart Glenn Greenwald, showed that "for the first time under the Obama Administration, the communications records of U.S. citizens are being collected indiscriminately and in bulk, regardless of whether they are suspected of wrongdoing."

One day later, on the 69th anniversary of the Normandy Invasion, the instantly infamous PRISM program was outed, where the NSA, in apparent agreement with nine major internet service providers (Google, Yahoo, Microsoft, Apple, YouTube et al), conducts warrantless electronic surveillance on virtually anybody at any NSA analyst's whim-97 *billion* pieces of intelligence were picked up worldwide in March 2013 alone.

The D-Day story leaker was an employee of private contractor Booz Allen Hamilton (owned by the Carlyle Group of George HW Bush and James Baker fame) named Edward Snowden. He was instantly and predictably demonized by the mainstream media in a knee-jerk attempt to shift focus away from the government's criminality. Forming a phalanx around its comedic congressional compadres, luminaries like MICMAC Mouthpiece Emeritus Tom Brokaw and wholly owed CBS subsidiary Bob Schieffer took to the airwaves to assure Americans "it's hard to make the case that our freedom has be compromised" (by NSA actions- Brokaw) and that "heroes don't run to China after putting the nation's security at risk." (Schieffer)

Fox trotted out Osama Bin Laden doppelganger Dick Cheney, still frightened to travel outside the U.S. because of an Interpol arrest warrant, who succinctly termed Snowden a "traitor," and it also helped keep the nation's attention focused on key issues like whether Snowden's girlfriend was or was not an actual pole-dancer.

The Ten Percent Approval Rating Congress has weighed in as well. Senator Lindsey "Cracker" Graham stated he was "glad" the NSA was tracking his calls, since he had "nothing to hide" because he wasn't a terrorist. Senator Dianne "I Feel" Feinstein called Snowden's act one of "treason," and Mike "It's a Beautiful Day in the Neighborhood" Rogers echoed Cheney with the "traitor" moniker. Rogers, who heads the House Intelligence Committee, gave a slightly ill-timed June 16 op-ed to the *Detroit Free Press* stating PRISM "cannot and does not monitor the communications of U.S. citizens." It was printed mere hours after the NSA itself admitted in a classified briefing that its analysts need no court authorization to listen to domestic phone calls or access the content of internet communications. All that's left for us is to find a nice resting place for the late Fourth Amendment.

Thomas Drake, the decorated Air Force and Navy veteran turned NSA whistleblower who was hounded by the Feds for four years until ten baseless felony charges were dropped against him, states that the illegal surveillance began promptly after 9/11. Known as operation Stellar Wind, the Bush Administration unilaterally decided to begin collecting data without warrants. The program's questionable legality was never an issue for the Bushies. "We just need the data," Drake was told by a superior. Bush simply signed a secret order authorizing blanket electronic surveillance. As Tricky Dick Nixon famously said, "When the President does it, that means that it's not illegal."

And when the NSA does it, it means that no one else knows about it. Of the individuals helping to destroy any semblance of what once made America the envy of all nations, perhaps none shines more brightly in his brass-buttoned uniform than four-star General Keith Alexander. A virtual law unto himself, Alexander now heads the NSA, U.S. Cyber Command, and the Central Security Service. He also is in charge of the Navy's 10th Fleet, 24th Air Force, and Second Army.

Though giving straight answers at congressional hearings has never been a high Alexander priority, complete U.S. military domination of cyberspace is. To further this goal, we now pay $30 billion per year to cyber security private contractors who help with the U.S. cyber offensive capabilities. (i.e. the 2006 Stuxnix raid damaging Iran's nuclear program). Unfortunately, these contractors are not prohibited from selling their expertise to foreign governments and/or front groups for terrorism. Thus, Alex and his minions have unwittingly set off a cyber arms race that puts U.S. infrastructure at greater risk than ever before.

We now classify 92 million documents for 1.4 million pairs of eyes. This is an increase from five million in 1995, eight million in 2001, and 16 million in 2005. Why not simply classify everything? That way, no questions need ever be answered by any government official. Barack "Mr. Transparency" Obama, an altogether worthy successor to Bush II in constitutional obliteration, has received fewer unrehearsed questions from the media than any modern president. But then, such queries were reportedly rare for Nero in the (original) 60s, too.

Chapter Seventeen

Welcome to the Truman Show (Part 1)

The true story of the commencement of the Cold War has been told, but not often enough. On February 27, 1947, present at the White House were Democratic President Harry Truman, Secretary of State George Marshall, Undersecretary Dean Acheson, and congressional leaders of both parties (Republicans controlled both Houses at the time). The immediate issue was whether or not the U.S. should step in where financially troubled Great Britain was bowing out – to help prop up a bungling Greece military regime that was, it was feared, in danger of being overthrown by communist insurgents. Never mind that there was no evidence (then or since) that the Soviet Union was supporting the rebels.

The congressional leaders were sensibly reluctant to commit large resources to a new Grecian formula. Marshall's plea for help went over like a lead zeppelin. *Then Acheson asked to speak.* The suave and articulate epitome of the Establishment (Groton, Yale, Covington & Burling) painted the world in stark black and white. Unbeknownst to all, the Soviets were taking it over. If Greece "fell", then the Middle East would be in jeopardy, then France and Italy, then . . . (different dominoes were later used with Vietnam).

The Congressional delegation qualifiedly capitulated. Michigan Senator Arthur Vandenberg told Truman, "Mr. President, the only way to get this program through is to make a speech to scare the hell out of the country." The President promptly obliged. But it was Acheson who had scared "hell" out of Vandenberg and Co. and, more than any other individual, architected the world in which we now live.

The resulting Truman Doctrine, announced March 12th, in effect stating the U.S. must fight communism wherever it was, led to the National Security Act, signed July 26th. This Act established the first peacetime intelligence agency, the CIA. In early 1950, National Security Council Report 68 (NSC-68) was presented to formalize the case that cataclysm would result should we not build up our military like Mark McGwire on steroids. At first Truman and key advisors rejected NSC-68's rationale. Then North Korea invaded South Korea. "The Korean War saved us,"* said Acheson later, meaning that the full might of U.S. resources would not have been used but for that conflict (ironically, many charged then Secretary of State Acheson with negligence for a speech he made omitting South Korea from the list of Far East countries that, if attacked, we would defend).

Truman signed NSC-68 into law that October. It was kept secret from the American public for a quarter century. It called for calculated and gradual coercion of the Soviet Union. Our military budget *quadrupled* over-

Our military budget *quadrupled* overnight.

night. In the Cold War years 1948 to 1991, over $15 trillion was spent (in 2004 dollars). We're still, paying, of course, interest on the debt it has left us.

The Soviet Union's collapse in 1991 also left us with a potential "peace dividend," but the defense spending gravy train was moving at too powerful a pace to be slowed down. One of its great legacies was (and is) the National Security Agency, which can be traced back to 1949. The NSA, a cryptologic intelligence organization which now illegally monitors domestic messages sent by U.S. citizens, was also kept secret from the U.S. public for a generation. A sampling of its list of historical achievements include: not knowing 100,000 North Korean troops were amassed at South Korea's border (1950), not having a clue that Soviet missiles were in Cuba (1962), no awareness of India's first nuclear test (1998), and no asking for an easily obtainable wiretap warrant when aware that two of the 9/11 hijackers were living near NSA headquarters in Maryland (2001).

When the NSA *has* performed credibly, like informing top brass that China was about to enter the Korean conflict (1950), the Tet offensive was about to happen in Vietnam (1968), or that Egypt and Syria were primed to attack Israel (1973), our Spy Guys have been ignored. The more pertinent question might be to ask: Who are the real Keystone Kops here? It can, in fairness, be argued that the NSA has outperformed the CIA, but the latter gang has a nearly unblemished record of ineptitude, excepting coups, that will be all-but-impossible to underperform.

In the Advanced Placement American History textbook my daughter used a mere two years ago, there is no mention of the National Security Act, NSC-68, or the National Security Agency. In the National Security State, 'tis better not to make the children aware now of what was kept hidden from their parents then. The Cold War has morphed into the "War on Terror." With the State controlling the remote, we watch the excitement without even having to change the channels ourselves.

-January 2010

---

*   But not the 33,629 Americans killed and 123,901 wounded in the 3 year stalemate.

(To be continued)

Mark J. Plawecki is a District Court Judge in Dearborn Heights. Confessions of a Condor offer a dissenting opinion on the current American status quo.

Chapter 18

Welcome to the Truman Show (Part 2)

"**W**e *accept the reality of the world with which we're presented.*" Thus spake Christoff, creator of *The Truman Show* in the 1998 movie of the same name. It is the story of Truman Burbank, who learns that, since his birth (when he became the first person to be legally adopted by a corporation), he has been living in a constructed reality TV show. With billions of viewers around the world observing his round-the-clock activities, he lives and works in a U.S. community that is actually a giant set, underneath a dome that doubles as the sky. His struggle to recognize, and then escape from, this encapsulation, forms the film's improbable plot.

Welcome to America 2010. The average citizen torpidly spends five hours per day watching TV. By one's 18th birthday, 350,000 commercials will have been seen, helping stunt any disinclination toward profligate consumerism. But with 24/7 news available, aren't we at least (potentially) well informed?

At World War II's end, 80% of all U.S. newspapers (where people used to get their news) were independently owned. Within two generations most had been gobbled up by giant chains. In 1983, alarm bells were heard when studies showed a mere 50 corporations owned 90% of what we watched, heard, or read. The Reagan Administration, though, thought regulations were too onerous on the behemoths. So by 1992, thanks to FCC rule changes allowing easier multiple ownership of media outlets, the number had to 23. All in the name of "free market" ideology.

Today the number is six. That's correct, fellow Burbanks . . . six megalithic monsters midwife 90% of all newspapers, magazines, TV stations, movies, records, videos, radio programming, and books we use. Only the "dangerous" (to Big Six profits) Internet provides hope. The Big Six are Disney (ABC as flagstaff), News Corp (Fox), Viacom (CBS), Time Warner (CNN), General Electric (NBC) and Bertelsmann (Random House Publishing).

"To make money is our only objective," says former Disney CEO Michael Eisner. Explains Viacom head Sumner Redstone, "When you make a movie for $10 million and then cross promote and sell it off of magazines, books, products, and TV shows out of your company, the profit potential is enormous." Indeed.

Last week I wrote of the Truman Administration and its consequences. In fairness, Give 'Em Hell Harry had compiled a record of achievement in the Senate, (enabling him to be a plausible running mate for FDR in '44), mainly by heading a committee exposing waste and corruption in the war profits industry. This was *during* World War II and under a Democratic Administration that had no wish to see its way of handling things scrutinized.

Today, we have the largest military budget, in real terms, since that war. President Obama has just proposed an additional $33 billion for Afghanistan and Iraq, with barely a peep from mainstream media, on top of the record $708 billion defense request for next fiscal year. The "waste and fraud" quote in this column's lead caption refers to private contractors in those two countries fleecing the American taxpayer. Senator Byron Dorgan should know. For five years now, he has headed the only committee in Washington investigating the abuse.

Unlike the Truman Committee, however, Dorgan's body has no subpoena or enforcement powers. Neither Republicans who controlled Congress before 2007, nor Democrats (since) have wanted it so. There is no interest in ferreting out waste. Unlike its World War II predecessor, today's Senate is too embedded with our military machine to upset a system which brings it the contributions needed to be re-elected. And there is no profit motive for the Big Six to tell Americans the truth. Hence, we're left in abject darkness.

When not complicit in covering up fraud, however, the Big Six happily continue to sell their favorite joint venture (with the government) product: Fear. How else to explain a potentially tragic but relatively minor incident like the Christmas Underbomber Attempt (with interesting allegations made by seemingly credible passengers – two Taylor, MI attorneys – being quickly suppressed from the mainstream "narrative") portrayed as yet another Pearl Harbor? Without debate, 450 full-body scanners will now be purchased for airport security folks' viewing pleasure and greater delays for air travelers.

In the 2000s decade, one passenger for every 25 million aboard a U.S. airliner (including 9/11) was killed by terrorists. Odds of being struck by lightning each year: one in 500,000. Yet we spend 50 times as much on homeland security as we do on the weather service. Why not a War on Lightning?

Citizens of the 38 most developed countries, reports the *Wall Street Journal,* have a one in three million chance of being killed by a terrorist; chance of being killed by a tornado – the same. How about a War on Twisters? Disney and Viacom, after they adopt the U.S. as the first wholly-owned corporate nation, ought to be able to make huge profits on these adventures. And they won't even have to cut God in for a percentage.

-January 2010

Mark J. Plawecki is a District Court Judge in Dearborn Heights. Confessions of a Condor pledges to continue a fondness for the quaint old U.S. Constitution.

Update 2013

The Truman Show, within its fictional framework, has no commercials. The "Show" is on air 24/7, and to keep it so advertising is done entirely by *product placement*. Corporate sponsors hope that the program's viewers will take note of the products touted by the characters and therefore think more strongly about using them themselves. Product placement has been present in movies and television for many years. The first such film Condor noted was 1982's *E.T.-The Extra Terrestrial*, featuring Reese's Pieces candy. The practice goes back, though, to at least the 1951 classic *The African Queen*, where Katherine Hepburn pours out all of Humphrey Bogart's Gordon's Gin bottles (Gordon's paid for this privilege) onto the dangerous river they are navigating.

In the real life Truman Show that has become modern America, product placement is ubiquitous. The bombardment of constant ads for the military-industrial complex consists not only of the literally millions of TV and radio commercials one is exposed to throughout an average life, but billboards which proliferate along main roads and highways reaching into the remotest areas of the country.

Things are no better online. No matter what website is visited, ads tailored to whatever our individual tastes might be instantly reach us. As internet guru Jaron Lainer frankly

> **"Spying on you is, for the moment, the official primary business of the information economy."**

admits, "Spying on you is, for the moment, the official primary business of the information economy."

However, certain products must not be placed where many might notice them, or at least deemphasized a much as possible. In America's Empire, four examples do nicely to demonstrate the strategy of maintaining the pose that we still live in a constitutional republic:

1. Cambodia- This tiny Southeast Asian country bordering Vietnam is vaguely remembered, four decades after U.S. troops left the latter nation, as a place of ancillary conflict. Most now know it as the home of the "Killing Fields" of the Khmer Rouge, which committed genocide on the Cambodian people.

The U.S. role in contributing to the horrors of the Khmer Rouge has never been mentioned by MICMAC media. Richard Nixon's 1970 illegal bombing campaign (then National Security Advisor Henry Kissinger infamously instructed General Alexander Haig "use anything that flies on anything that moves") is known, but the extent to which Cambodia was terrorized is not.

Documents released by the Clinton Administration in 2000 indicate the massiveness of the bombing of this impoverished and essentially defenseless nation, even before Nixon took office. From 1965 to 1973 over 2.7 million tons of U.S. bombs rained on Cambodia, contrasted with 2 million tons dropped by the Allies in *all* of World War II. This makes Cambodia the most heavily bombed nation in history. And it was technically a neutral state during the Vietnam War. A significant amount of ordnance is still unexploded, making vast areas of its agricultural land unusable.

2. Diego Garcia- This tiny island in the Indian Ocean was owned by the United Kingdom. Its inhabitants, the Chagossians, were descendants of African and Indian slaves. By the late 1950s the U.S. military had developed a Cold War policy of acquiring as many foreign bases as possible. Persistent deceptions of Congress and other governmental officials, spanning many years, enabled the Navy to acquire the island from the British. This included allowing the Brits to do the dirty work of deporting the island's 2000 inhabitants-they were dumped on the coasts of Mauritius and Seychelles, some 1200 miles away.

The base has been kept secret for generations, though leaks from an authoritative a source as retired four-star General Barry McCaffrey has acknowledged its use as a detention center (i.e. "black site") for holding War on Terror prisoners. It was also used as a launch pad for bombers in both the Iraq and Afghan wars.

The Chagossians have sought legal redress to return home (even to islands 135 miles away from the base), and a British high court in 2000 agreed that their deportation was illegal. However, the UK simply issued an executive order in 2004 abolishing the natives' rights to live in the land of their birth. This was at the height of Prime Minister Tony "The Poodle" Blair's subservience-to- George W. Bush-routine in the GWOT. Britain's highest court, in 2008, voted 3-2 to declare Chagossian rights unimportant when the U.S. had decided it needed the island lest terrorists put it to evil use.

In 2010 Wikileaks cables revealed that, in order to quash any Chagossian refugee petitions, Diego Garcia would be made a permanent marine reserve. This environmental designation would in no way affect the 3000 to 5000 U.S. military personnel stationed there-just former inhabitants begging to come back. David Vine's *Island of Shame*, from which the above is largely taken, documents *sixteen* such instances of local populations displaced for U.S. base expansion.

3. Guantanamo-Unlike Cambodia and Diego Garcia, most Americans are aware of the detention camp where 779 "terrorists" were placed by the Bush Administration in 2002. They are less aware, though, that approximately 600 have been released, many after years of detention, without charges. If they were the "worst of the worst," as Defense Secretary Donald Rumsfeld claimed, then the Bush cabal didn't see Americans' safety an especially high priority.

Of the 166 who remain, six have been charged. Contrast this farcical fact with the 578 *non*-Guantanamo cases that have been brought since 9/11 in U.S. federal courts, with an average delay until trial of only 1.4 years (it's 7.8 years in military tribunal cases). Eighty-six of the 166 prisoners were scheduled for release as of June 2013, but Congress will not let them go.

Barack Obama campaigned for president promising to close the "shameful" facility, and upon taking office signed an order to close it within one year. Nearly five years have passed since the signing; there is no end to "Gitmo" in sight. There is a possible end, though, to many of the prisoners (80% of whom were not picked up "on the battlefield" as the Bush Administration originally claimed, but rather as $5000 bounties by Pakistan and Afghan warlords whose interest in the U.S. War on Terror was questionable at best). Over 100 have been engaged in a lengthy hunger strike to protest conditions and their continual imprisonment.

4. War College- In May 2012, *Wired Magazine* reported that an instructor at the Department of Defense's Joint Forces Staff College at National Defense University was advocating the destruction, by nuclear means, of Mecca and Medina (both in Saudi Arabia; they are the two holiest cities in Islam), plus total war on Islam. Lt Colonel Matthew Dooley insisted that there was no such thing as "moderate Islam, and so the U.S. options were to pulverize the religion into "cult status," or surrender. Events were proving, according to Dooley, that there is no viable third way.

Dooley had taught hundreds of officers from four service branches, and school commandment major General Joseph Ward reportedly approved the class material. Pentagon top brass, when receiving information about the class, suspended it and assigned Dooley elsewhere. Less than one year later, Dooley was threatening to sue the Pentagon for receiving a negative performance review.

News of the class hit international media. None of the major U.S. broadcasters (ABC, NBC, CBS, CNN, or Fox*) deemed it worthy of a mention. This obviously would not be good product placement for a MICMAC insisting it has no pretentions to Empire.

-July 2013

---

* *FoxNews.com did eventually report Dooley's suspension from teaching in October 2012. It incorrectly stated that "Muslim groups" caused the Pentagon's actions, and, of course, made no mention of the inflammatory advocacy and materials. Self-proclaimed "fair and balanced," Fox never misses an opportunity to bury truth whenever possible.*

Chapter Nineteen

Love among the Ruins

"Who collects what money from whom in order to spend on what is all there is to politics, and in a serious country should be a preoccupation of the media."

- Gore Vidal

For this column Condor is joined again by predecessor Spartacus and their errantly erudite pal Boethius. The Place: Bankrupt America's new epicenter: Grosse Pointe Shores, MI. The Time: Super Bowl XILV (The Year of Rozelle 2010 for non-Romans).

Sparty: Hey, what gives with Grosse Pointe Shores, not long ago the nation's seventh wealthiest enclave and still third richest city in Michigan?

Bo: On the watch list for receivership, I'm afraid. Joining the likes of Detroit, Highland Park, Ecorse and, due to the commercial real estate collapse, Troy.

Sparty: But how is it possible that this blissful bastion of busy bees and blessed billionaires is in serious financial trouble?

Condor: According to reports, $16.6 million in unfunded pension and healthcare liabilities. But ask our host, Super CPA/Lawyer and Shores councilman Thaddeus Kedzierski. Political newcomer Ted noticed something was wrong with the city's financial books, and is making residents aware. Don't be too concerned about GPS though; such crises are happening in cities across the country. Los Angeles may be bankrupt by summer.

Bo: Too bad Ted isn't employed as watchdog for Pentagon spending.

Sparty:	Guys, I'm seeing "Obama Socialism" bumper stickers on my drives to the bread lines.
Condor:	As our pen pal Tommy K begins every letter now, "Be careful, you might get what you voted for."
Sparty:	We voted for a Bush Third Term?
Bo:	Tommy likes to remind us of our failure to understand that President John McCain was fully prepared to save the nation from the policies Senator John McCain had espoused since Super Bowl XVIII (1984).
Sparty:	The Raiders beat Washington that year . . . and Washington's been raiding us since. Why isn't Condor watching the game?
Bo:	Boycotting it, for 10th consecutive year. You see, football replaced baseball as America's most popular sport in 1968, the Year of Super Bowl II. Condor thinks it no coincidence that the country's serious financial woes began to alarmingly mount that year. Funding two wars (on Poverty and Vietnam) at once is always an expensive enterprise. Not to mention electing Nixon.
Sparty:	If Con figures America won't bounce back 'til baseball reclaims the top spot in U.S. hearts and minds, we're in HUGE trouble. He'll need intervention from the mythological Graces to make that happen. Today's game may be the most watched event ever (Editor's note: It was.)
Bo:	"We didn't get here overnight." I learned in Lansing last week. That goes for the nation as well. For instance, in 1975. . .
Sparty:	You mean the Year of Super Bowl IX, Pittsburgh over Minnesota. . .
Bo:	I mean the year the top 148 U.S. corporations paid $10 billion in U.S. taxes and $20 billion to foreign governments. The top eight "American" banks all showed a profit, yet none paid taxes.

Sparty: Precursor to 2008, huh? We should have Transparency Ted explain that one. But he's busy hobnobbing with Ralph Wilson and/or Doug Hamel.

Condor: Our corporations now pay 12 percent of all federal revenues. In the 1950s, they averaged 28 percent.

Bo: Plus they've received an early Valentine's Day gift from the Supremes' Fab Five. *Citizens United v Federal Election Commission* says big corporations can spend unlimited funds to buy, er, I mean support preferred political candidates. Foreign corporations, too.

Sparty: Speaking of Valentine's Day, wasn't this Super Bowl the closest in time to February 14?

Condor: Correct, Spartamo. Bo thought it apropos to merge "the celebration of love and affection between intimate companions." In this case America and the NFL.

Bo: A look at Friday's national corporate comic-strip, *The USA Today* shows...

Sparty: It was super cool! XXXIV of its LIV pages devoted to sports and entertainment, XXVI to sports alone, and XX on The Game. I'd say proper priorities on display.

Condor: "Bread and circuses," reminds a wise Federal judge-in-waiting. But it's going to end in 19 months.

Sparty: Say it ain't so, Bo!

Bo: Condor's right. The NFL owners are going to lock out the players. Their $5 billion guaranteed TV revenues aren't enough to keep profits at acceptable levels. So the players will have to spend 2011 like their NHL brethren did in 2004 -2005.*

Sparty: And you think the Tea Partiers are mad now...

Bo: Actually, the NFL is the most successful form of socialism in world history. Don't forget, all the TV revenue is divided equally between the teams. So every one (except, by secret charter agreement, the Lions) has a

	chance at success. As Art Modell once noted, "We NFL owners are 32 Republicans who vote socialist."
Sparty:	Well, that pinko-commie lock-out's not gonna play well in Pete Hoekstra's Holland, or even the People's Republic of Ann Arbor.
Condor:	(smiling) I know... maybe then We the People will put the Summer Game back on top. If only Fox will keep the contests under four hours.
Bo:	With its Steroid Era exposed and hopefully over, Maddux's amazing achievements acquire an even greater luster. Hey, STOP GLANCING AT THE SAINTS' TOUCHDOWNS, BOYCOTT CHEATER!
Sparty:	He can't help it. Ted has nine televisions.
Condor:	Anyway, with his career earnings completely saved, maybe Mad Dog can help bail out LA. After all, he did end his playing days pitching in relief for the Dodgers.

Judge Mark J. Plawecki serves on the bench of the Wayne County 20th District Court. *Confessions of a Condor* offers a dissenting view of today's Establishment. Plawecki is president of the Polish American Legal Society (PALS), an association of friendly attorneys. It is currently quite solvent, reports its longtime treasurer...Thaddeus "Ted" Kedzierski.

-February 2010

---

* The owners did lock out the players for 4 ½ months in 2011 but, perhaps fearing mass revolution from a NFL-obsessed populace, settled in late July with a new ten year agreement to save the season and presumably next decade.

Rigging America

Condor read *The Last Mafioso* while an undergrad in the early 1980s. Because of the corruption revealed therein, he vowed never to spend a dime in a casino (Vegas or elsewhere), a promise kept to this day. In retrospect, he would have been wiser to have pledged to keep his retirement account out of the hands of Wall Street financial types. But life remains a slow learning process.

A growing list of U.S. cities is now termed "near bankruptcy." Three municipalities in California have recently filed, with Stockton in 2012 becoming the country's largest to ever so declare. These follow on the heels of Harrisburg, PA, and Jefferson County, Ala (both 2011), the latter home to the largest default ever, at $4.2 billion. Approximately 75% of Jefferson's debt was entangled in a crooked sewer reconstruction project and subsequent bond swap deal financed by JP Morgan Chase, which ended up being penalized a paltry $75 million for its "unlawful payment scheme" (i.e. bribery).

Detroit is reportedly next, and has had an emergency manager in place since March 2013. It will easily surpass Stockton as the largest city bankruptcy (almost assuredly not if but) when the filing occurs. Gross mismanagement has undoubtedly played a significant role in Detroit's (and the others') situation. However, via a 2012 federal court case, we now have incontrovertible evidence that Wall Street has been skimming untold billions of dollars from government entities all across America.

The scam works as follows: Whenever a city, county, state, authority, hospital, school, district, etc. decides to enact a building project, it scurries to Wall Street for financing. Wall Street firms sell bonds to investors, and these bonds then enable the governmental body to pay contractors as work begins to get done on the project.

However, not all payments are due at once, as projects can take years to complete. In the meantime, the money raised by the entity needs to be invested. The best interest rate possible is naturally desired. So *auctions* are held, where banks ostensibly compete to win the bond investment.

We found out in 2012, though, that the auctions are rigged. The case of *U.S. v Carollo, Goldberg, and Grimm* revealed that the big banks-JP Morgan Chase, Bank of America, UBS, Goldman Sachs, GE Capital (the finance arm of GE), and others take turns "winning" auctions at rates lower than what would have been paid in an honest contest. The winning bid turns out to be "just over" the others, because the winner is told ahead of time by a bribed auctioneer what the other bids are.

So, for example, if a bank were willing to pay 6% interest, and it learns that the other two bids are 5% and 5.25%, it will bid 5.3% or 5.5%, and pocket the difference between what it pays and what it might have been willing to pay. In *U.S. v Carollo*, one deal cheated Allegheny County, PA out of "only" about $88,000 per year. But multiply this by thousands of deals that make up the $3.7 *trillion* muni-bond market, and you get an idea of the enormity of the theft.

The *Carollo* trial was brilliantly documented by *Rolling Stone's* Matt Taibbi in "The Scam Wall Street Learned from the Mafia" (June 21, 2012). Bank of America and JP Morgan Chase paid a combined $365 million in penalties but were rewarded with $3.5 billion each in 2011 public deals. Taibbi: "Get busted for welfare fraud even once in America, and good luck getting so much as a food stamp ever again. Get caught rigging interest rates in 50 states, and the government goes right on handing you billions of dollars in public contracts."

One of the defendants in the *Carollo* case testified that then-New Mexico Bill Richardson, who was seeking the Democratic presidential nomination, accepted $100,000 (including an envelope stuffed with $25,000 in cash) in exchange for giving the defendant's firm a $1.5 million contract with his state. Richardson's nomination as Barack Obama's Commerce Secretary was withdrawn when a grand jury first investigated the affair.

Another egregious political establishment connection occurred when JP Morgan Chase CEO Jamie Dimon was called before the House Finance Committee in June 2012 to explain how Chase had just lost what turned out to be at least $5.8 billion in derivatives trades. Dimon was treated deferentially by Committee Chair Spencer Bachus (R-Ala), who insisted his guest *not* testify under oath (hence no perjury charge could result). Chase had doled out $374,355 to committee members-three times its next largest committee donation-and $119,000 to Bachus alone, making them his second biggest contributor. But then Bachus, who has opposed reform at every instance, once famously admitted he was there "to serve the banks." Adding insult, Bachus represents the aforementioned Jefferson County, which Chase greatly helped guide into bankruptcy.

The last line of the hilarious movie spoof *Airplane!* terms municipal bonds America's "best investment." For Wall Street mobsters, they certainly are. The game's been rigged, reminiscent of the Mafia's skimming from Vegas casinos in the days of Jimmy Fratianno. Only now Nevada's gambling tourists aren't the only poor suckers-all of us outside Wall Street are. A beautiful system-for the ultimate cake-eaters-remains largely intact.

-July 2013

Chapter Twenty

Anniversary Month

Last month's annual Michigan Judicial Conference has shaken Condor from his (seemingly 500) Days of Summer doldrums. Approximately that many legal scholars sans their black robes gathered in a rebirthing of JFK's Jefferson. In other words, there was, despite the absences of Kenny* and Sullivan, the finest collection of minds assembled at the Amway Grand since Van Andel and DeVos devised, or didn't, the Ponzi scheme alone. The conference concluded (providentially, Judge Warren might say) 223 years to the day after the epochal ending of the Constitutional Convention in Philadelphia, now home to renowned federal law expert Michael Vick. In this brave new world of fiscal austerity, we jurists pledged our lives and sacred honor to ensure our fortunes won't be taken, at least without a domestic donnybrook.

But enough boasting of those who independently declare to protect the Constitution and lesser documents. Next September 11 will be the 10th anniversary of the al-Qaeda attacks on U.S. soil, and if this year's commemorative events were indicators, it is safe to say 9/11 is our new Unequaled Day of Remembrance, to make sure We the People don't forget why we dispossessed 4.5 million non-al-Qaeda Iraqis from their homes, caused the death of hundreds of thousands in this same nation, and are now, despite our best intelligence estimates of "50 to 100" al-Qaeda operatives in Afghanistan, not only not leaving that country anytime soon, but, in the words of Comic of Defense Robby Gates, "not ever leaving at all." And there are those who keep fretting about not bequeathing anything for future generations . . .

There are several more anniversary dates which, had you been paying attention only to corporatized media, you may not have been made aware:

September 4 — the 15 year anniversary of the rape and near killing of a 12 year old Japanese girl on Okinawa, by two U.S. marines and one sailor. This incident, because the three perpetrators made it back to their base, and our Status of Forces Agreement with Japan allows us to keep suspects out of Japanese police control, led to the largest anti-American demonstrations in Okinawa's history. Isolated incident? Between 1998 and 2004, 1706 reported U.S. servicemen crimes or accidents resulted in no disciplinary measures. A grand total of one led to a court-martial.

Today, 38 U.S. bases still control nearly 20 percent of Okinawa's land. Eighty-five percent of this island's natives oppose the U.S. presence there, 65 years after the end of World War II but, well, see the above Gates remark.

September 16 — the 25th, or Silver Year, since the U.S. Commerce Department declared America, for the first time since 1914, a debtor nation. Twenty five stellar seasons of adding debt has brought us now, at last, to the brink of bankruptcy. It has also handed us a real unemployment rate not seen since before Pearl Harbor.

September 18 — Two years since the infamous meeting where Hammerin' Hank Paulsen and Ben "Bugsy" Bernanke browbeat Washington's top elected officials into believing that imminent collapse awaited us should they not immediately bailout the big banks who caused the panic in the first place. All Americans can take pride in knowing that the taxpayer bailout has returned these banks to enormous profitability, and any complaints about them not loaning money to the rest of us is really just sour grapes.

September 30 — the 60th annual marker of the Official Beginning of the National Security State. The old Republic was quietly retired this date by President Truman's signing of NSC - 68, the classified blueprint for winning the Cold War. Unfortunately, once we won, no one bothered to write a new blueprint. Two decades later, our military continues growing as a lymphoma throughout the body politic, and anyone who doubts its power as The Decider need only check Gossip-in-Chief Bob Woodward's latest quotefest— *Washington Post* excerpts will do (Obama: Generals, I said provide me three Afghan options. Generals: Sir, we thought we'd spare you the trouble, since this is the one you're going to choose).

America can no longer afford its empire. However, until more of its citizenry become aware that they reside in one (the notion is still taboo in corporate media), it will continue to defend its interests, defined as anything on Planet Earth (not to mention space), against any threat — real, perceived, or invented.

> **...until more of its citizenry become aware that they reside in one...**

Analytical documentation of this view arrived in 2010 in a trio of splendid books: Garry Wills' *Bomb Power*; *Washington Rules* by Andrew Bacevich; and Chalmers Johnson's *Dismantling the Empire*.

Johnson, the author of the Blowback Trilogy (the first of which warned us of a 9/11- type attack), calls for abolishment of the disastrous CIA. Bacevich, a former Army colonel now teaching at Boston University, defines the sacred trinity of U.S. foreign policy as "global military presence, global power projection, and global interventionism." The incomparable Wills, who traces our empire to the birth of the Atomic Bomb, has been predictably ignored by "mainstream" colleagues, as he was last year by Obama when, invited to the White House, he advised The Prez to deescalate the Afghan madness.

The Establishment's disregarding its preeminent intellectuals' warnings gives ample reason to check out one or more of this timely tome trifecta. Another is provided by the simple yet startling fact that time is rapidly running out.

-October 2010

---

* Timothy M. Kenny, arguably (with Robert J. Colombo, Jr.) metropolitan Detroit's finest trial court judge.

Mark J. Plawecki is a District Court Judge in Dearborn Heights. This September 16 also marked the 22-year wedding anniversary of the author and Ms. Julie — The Empire's Elementary School Teacher Extraordinaire.

A Cold Warrior Turned Hot against Empire

Chalmers Johnson died on November 20, 2010, age 79, from complications of rheumatoid arthritis. In his life's last decade, four wake-up call books were published for what he termed a "somnolent" American public: *Blowback* (2000), *Sorrows of Empire* (2004), *Nemesis* (2006), and *Dismantling the Empire* (2010). This quadruple warning reflected Johnson's growing alarm over the curious U.S. retreat from a republican form of government into one where a military dictatorship seems increasingly likely. The political scientist in Johnson made him profess, by 2007, that it was probably "far too late" to alter our course. Nevertheless, he battled in print and via interviews for the Republic right up until his end.

Johnson enlisted in the U.S. Navy during the Korean War. He could have used his arthritic condition, diagnosed in his early 20s, to avoid military service, but refused. After obtaining bachelor's, masters, and doctorate degrees from the University of California, Berkeley, he went on to teach at his alma mater for a quarter century, and then also at UC-San Diego.

He made his name originally as an authority on East Asian affairs, particularly China and Japan. His expertise in this area was so renowned that Harvard offered him a position on its faculty in 1982. He turned down the invitation after a visit there, telling his wife, "They want me as a moose-head professor-to hang my head on the wall and say they've bagged me." One senses that an anti-elitist streak ran deeply in the Phoenix AZ native.

As a consultant to the CIA under Richard Helms (from 1967-1973), "Chal" saw up close the incompetence of an organization that convinced him the U.S. didn't have an intelligence service, just a "private army to the President." Still, he remained a cold warrior through the end of the Soviet Union, which he had thought of, he said in 2007, "as a menace, and still do."

His change regarding U.S. foreign policy came after the Soviet Union's collapse in 1991. He expected, as did many, a "peace dividend" since the *raison d'etre* for our gargantuan

A New Enemy had to be found.

military spending to that point had suddenly vanished. But the vested interests had become too ingrained. The Pentagon began to speak of "full spectrum dominance." A New Enemy had to be found. "China, terrorism, drug lords, anything, even instability," said Johnson. The 9/11 attacks proved the perfect rationale to ratchet up the workings of MICMAC.

Johnson saw striking similarities between the late Roman Republic and our present predicament. The Roman Senate handed over power to the Emperor, much as our Congress has to the "imperial presidency." Rome's 35 major military bases at its height of domination nearly pars with the 40 U.S. biggies now spread throughout the globe. The 737 *total* foreign bases Johnson called attention to (since grown to over 1000) by itself assures a lasting gratitude from a previously unaware citizenry.

Through the Eye of a Needle, Peter Brown's recent magisterial study of the Roman Empire at its dissolution stage, points to perhaps even more telling parallels. The money spent to maintain its vast empire proved such a drain on its treasury that the rich began shifting the burden of taxation to the poor. Tax evaders under the Emperor Valentinian III in 441 CE evinced the same rhetoric corporate media now gives to multinational corporations who report U.S. losses while earning enormous foreign profits and contribute nothing to the U.S. Treasury (many in fact receive refunds).

Additionally, as the structures of society collapsed in the late Roman Empire, solidity in the outlying cities of Africa and Gaul was achieved by the roar of the circus. "Altogether, to go to the cities in a time of crisis was not to succumb to luxury but to show a robust, civic patriotism," writes Brown.

Today, as Detroit crumbles, so long as the baseball team has a good chance of returning to the World Series, $180 million in expenditures to maintain a star pitcher is inherently acceptable, without a trace of irony, to an elite devising ways to reduce the pensions of modest income retirees. Now, as then, "to love one's city was to love the games."

Chalmers Johnson is part of Condor's personal pantheon of contemporary writers whose influence has been greatest. He is a member of what I call the "Elite Eleven," * and I would single out *Nemesis* as his best work. Actually, a 52 minute monologue (Google Chalmers Johnson on American Hegemony) is a great introduction to his last decade's thought. If Americans were more interested in reality instead of reality TV, this succinct critique of MICMAC would be required viewing for every high school senior.

-July 2013

---

*   The others, alphabetically, accompanied by their most influential (for me) book, are Andrew Bacevich (*Washington Rules*), Rene Girard (*Things Hidden Since the Foundation of the World*), Chris Hedges (*Empire of Illusion*), Naomi Klein (*The Shock Doctrine*), Bill McKibben (*Eaarth*), William Pfaff (*The Irony of Manifest Destiny*), Kevin Phillips (*Bad Money*), Gore Vidal (*United States*), Garry Wills (*Confessions of a Conservative*), and Howard Zinn (*A People's History of the United States*).

Chapter Twenty-one

Twin Attacks II

"It is dangerous to be right when the government is wrong."

– Voltaire

The release by WikiLeaks of U.S. State Department cables demonstrating quite clearly the criminal elements ensconced in our federal government coincides nicely with the even more transparently visible fact that the current regime has proven, once and for all, to be a puppet of, by, and for the rich.

Date Which Will Live in Infamy II saw Julian Assange arrested in London for having sex without a condom in Sweden, Reno apparently being temporarily unavailable. Also, this December 7 witnessed a joint sneak attack by Republicans in Congress with Capitulator-in-Chief Barack Obama on the U.S. budget, capsizing it $900 billion so we perhaps won't ever forget the USS Arizona.

Never mind that top marginal tax rates over 90 percent were in vogue when our Empire was economically thriving (in the days of Truman-Eisenhower-Kennedy). Now the wealthiest 2 percent of us can't live without an extension of a decade-long rate of 35 percent; an onerous increase to 39.6 percent loomed in McMansionland's front windows. Instantly forgotten in this farce is the Democrats' nixed second proposal (after the first one of increasing rates only on $250,000-plus households failed), which would have extended the cuts on the first $1 million of every single American. But then what's a multimillionaire to do? Thus Obama guarantees a serious primary challenge in 2012 from an actual Democrat.*

The arrest of Assange on dubious sex charges fools no one this side of Eric "The Red" Holder. Assange has now been made Empire Enemy No. 1 by its apologists for, well, exposing the truth. The federal assault on WikiLeaks is a desperate message from the bowels of the imperial regime: Don't mess with us, or else. Calls for Assange's assassination (former Canadian PM Harper's aide), or being "hunted down like bin Laden" (Sarah the Polar Tweet) to being charged with espionage (Dianne "Einstein" Feinstein) show the tyrannical impulse at Empire Establishment's core.

Nowhere in our "free" (meaning non-Internet) press is anything resembling truth being told. The facts are that WikiLeaks has worked with five major papers of international notoriety, including the *New York Times*, and has so far released less than 1,000 of the 251,297 cables given it by a U.S. government whistleblower. These papers have all published numerous cables, after coordinated (between WikiLeaks and the papers) redactions to protect innocent people. WikiLeaks had actually previously approached the State Department to help it in the redactions, but State refused. Bad move.

The cables have shown, yet again, a foreign policy of high comedy and higher corruption. In the former Soviet satellites Turkmenistan and Kazakhstan, for example, we wholeheartedly support ruthless dictators who keep their populations in abject poverty. Turkmen leader Gurbanguly Berdimuhamedov profits handsomely from having the world's largest natural gas reserves. Our cable guy: "Berdi does not like people smarter than he is. Since he's not a very bright person, he is suspicious of a lot of people."

In Kazakhstan, leader Nursultan Nazarbayev holds the world's largest oil reserves. In his latest election two top political opponents committed suicide by shooting themselves in the back of the head, then binding their own hands behind their backs. Clever Cossacks were they! Needless to say, Nursu and Berdi are two of our staunch allies in the "War on Terror."

The cables also reveal that al Qaeda is safely harbored and/or funded by Saudi Arabia, Kuwait, and the United Arab Emirates—more close U.S. allies. Meanwhile, the maiming of Iraq and Afghanistan continue, to the delight of our giant defense contractors. And though Hillary Clinton orders illegal spying and theft of UN officials' personal information, the wrath of Wolf Blitzer, heard from both CNN and the Romulan neutral zone, centers on why We the People (and he) are allowed to even learn about it. Strange journalism Wolf digested at the *Jerusalem Post*.

The battle lines have been demarcated in the first genuine cyber war — between those who believe in democracy, and the imperial class personified by Joe "Shut down the Internet" Lieberman, a man whose twin loyalties to the Israel and insurance industries are above reproach. Democracy is a concept Uncle Joe has managed to purge from a troubled intellect now haunted by a political career of near perfect perfidy. As Assange wrote four years ago, "The more secretive or unjust an organization is, the more leaks induce fear and paranoia in its leadership and planning coterie." Washington, look in thy mirror.

But the government will lose this war. Already, more than 500 copies of the embarrassing documents are on different web sites. As Condor noted in these pages in January, the Internet, flawed as it may be, is the only hope left for the dissemination of truth in our corporate media controlled society. By prosecuting Assange, Lieberman & Co. might unwittingly be cutting their own throats.

-December 2010

---

*   Perhaps Condor's poorest prognostication of Obama's first term.

The Remarkable, Unfathomable Silence of Truman Show Media

> "America does not have a functioning democracy at this point in time."
>
> – Jimmy Carter,
> *July 16, 2013*

To opine that U.S. mainstream media (MSM) is poll-obsessed might be considered an understatement. Polls about virtually everything are taken, then reported; the now round-the-cycle presidential polls concerning Who's Ahead Three Years Plus for Election 2016 is as annoying (and useless) a time-filler as can be found (CBS, CNN, ABC, NBC, and Fox have all reported these in the last two months).

So it was perhaps revelatory to see the Quinnipiac Polling Institute (regularly cited by all of MSM) poll released July 10 regarding leaker of NSA secrets Edward Snowden. Despite over a month of barrages from the Obama Administration, leaders of both parties in Congress, and MSM talking heads, Americans by a 55-34% margin thought Snowden more "whistleblower" than "traitor." Perhaps the TV exes who, in effect, collude with our government to manufacture nightly news were slightly disturbed. Why else, while widely disseminated on the internet, did not a single one of the CBS, CNN, ABC, NBC, or Fox giants remember to mention this poll? Were they all simply taking a day away from polling to give their continuously dwindling viewership a break?

David Gregory, host of the most watched Sunday news talk show *Meet the Press*, had led the brigade. Interviewing Glenn

Greenwald, who had initially reported the story told to him by Snowden, Gregory demanded, "To the extent you aided and abetted Mr. Snowden, why shouldn't you be charged with a crime?"

To this "To the extent you beat your wife" query Greenwald responded by denying Gregory's premise-that he had aided or abetted Snowden-and that under it "every investigative journalist in the United States who works with their sources, who received classified information, is a criminal."

Actually, if had watched the show from its beginning, Greenwald could have asked Sir David the same question. Gregory had referred to a secret FISA court opinion and "people I have talked to" regarding it. As Trevor Timm writes, "Does Gregory think he should be charged with a crime for talking to sources asking questions about classified information, then reporting what he learned?" Except that when *Gregory* leaks classified information, it's invariably from a *government* source who wants the information released.

Greenwald has been vilified in Truman Show media, but it has been upset with him for some time. In 2009, he was named co-winner of the I.F. Stone Award for Independent (i.e.-non-toadying to the Establishment) Journalism. This is why corporate shills like Gregory can question his "journalistic" credentials.

In October 2012, Greenwald reacted to a post-presidential debate interview a Florida Congresswoman gave with arguably the most accurate headline of the entire campaign- "The remarkable, unfathomable ignorance of Debbie Wasserman Shultz." In the interview (available on YouTube) Wasserman Shultz was asked if she would be comfortable with Mitt Romney having a "Kill List" similar to the current one President Obama has. She stated she had never heard of such a thing, reported on since 2010 and centerpiece of a 600 word, front page expose in the *New York Times* in May 2012. She said she'd answer any "serious" questions the stunned interviewer had, thus clearly giving the impression she was oblivious to, as a sitting member of Congress and also Chair of the

Democratic National Committee, one of the biggest stories of this Administration.

CNN, ABC, CBS, and Fox have all interviewed Wasserman Schultz since this gaffe; not one reporter has ever mentioned it. On May 26, 2013, ABC's *This Week* went so far as to have her as part of its "powerhouse roundtable," as an expert on...*our drone policy* (Condor is not making this up).

President Carter's quote at top came during an Atlanta-based interview with German weekly *Der Spiegel*. Carter offered support for Snowden's actions, which was promptly reported in the international media. But nary a mention from our Truman Show friends.

The common thread of these events is the willingness of U.S. corporate-owned media to keep the citizenry from knowing any story that might shed light on its sycophantic role with those in power. Ronald Unz of *The American Conservative* relates ("Our American Pravda," April 29, 2013) this chilling antedote regarding the late Russian oligarch Boris Berezovsky, reputedly the power behind President Boris Yeltsin in the 1990s:

"According to the *New York Times,* he had planned to transform Russia into a fake two-party state, one social-democratic and one neoconservative-in which heated public battles would be fought on divisive, symbolic issues, while behind the scenes both parties would actually be controlled by the same ruling elites...Given America's history over the last two decades, perhaps we can guess where Berezovsky got his idea for such a clever political scheme."

As cable news feeds us nothing less than nauseous amounts of detail concerning the George Zimmerman Trial and its aftermath, a "divisive, symbolic" issue known as race is serving America's oligarchs quite well indeed.

-August 2013

Chapter Twenty-two

Ike's Warning at Fifty

Today marks the 50th anniversary of President Dwight Eisenhower's Farewell Address. This 1961 speech of profound prescience contains the following: "In the councils of government, we must guard against the acquisition of unwarranted influence, whether sought or unsought, by the military-industrial complex. The potential for the disastrous rise of misplaced power exists and will persist."

Eisenhower had been formulating his remarks since at least May 1959. One draft had him referring to the "military-industrial-congressional complex"; he had originally hoped to give the speech before Congress, and thought it might be bad form to harangue his hosts. Ike should have kept in the third element — the invitation from Capitol Hill never came.

Ten years after Eisenhower's address, Senator J. William Fulbright (whose scholarship program became the largest educational exchange curriculum in history) wrote the all-but-suppressed *The Pentagon Propaganda Machine*. The longest serving chair of the Senate Foreign Relations Committee opined, "For almost twenty years now, many of us in Congress have more or less blindly followed our military spokesmen. Some have become captive of the military. We are on the verge of becoming a military nation." He also thought that our public policy's greatest danger lay in civilian authorities adopting the "narrowness of outlook of professional soldiers."

In between Eisenhower's adios and Fulbright's book, then Commander of the U.S. Marine Corps General David Shoup stated "America has become a militaristic and aggressive nation."

That was four and five decades ago. Today, our military has so completely metastasized over our nation's body that it imperils our soul. The $2.75 million military spending limit for public relations Congress lifted in 1959 has now grown to $5 *billion* per annum.

Military growth itself is regarded as reduction. Chief Orwellian media outlet *The Wall Street Journal* on January 7 headlined page one with "Pentagon Faces the Knife," the spin being that Defense Secretary Robert Gates' proposed $78 billion shift from obsolete to more useful programs over the next five years was somehow a cut. The story admitted, in its fourth paragraph, that Gates' outlined plans didn't "include an actual decrease in the military budget. But it will stop growing by 2015." Perhaps implicit in the article is the proposition that Americans don't peruse past paragraph three in stories anymore. (If true, then only Judge Allen is reading these and the words to follow.)*

Eisenhower's fears have come to fruition. There are more than 47,000 prime contractors doing Department of Defense work, with more than 100,000 subcontractors in tow, making for a massive conglomerate penetrating nearly all sectors of society. "The Pentagon's payroll is a veritable who's who of the top companies in the world," writes Nick Turse in *The Complex*. Virtually all aspects of American life, from entertainment and sports to basic consumer goods and education, are interconnected with our military.

> **"The Pentagon's payroll is a veritable who's who of the top companies in the world."**

And how do these companies win contracts? More than ever before, they use the revolving door of Washington to dizzying success. *The Boston Globe* recently ran an in-depth study of 750 retired generals and admirals who feast on government largesse for defense firms. Eighty to ninety percent of these three-and four star-ry knights went to work for firms lobbying for DoD contracts, and most were recruited well before they left the government.

The general in charge of our Air Force weapons systems, in fact, upon retirement immediately went to shill for Northrop Grumman (manufacturer of the B-2 stealth bomber) as a paid consultant and joined a top-secret Pentagon study program on stealth aircraft technology. No conflict there, say Pentagon brass.

The Pentagon's bureaucracy is so huge that even *it* doesn't know how many offshore bases it has. Nicholas Kristoff 's December 26 *New York Times* column, relying on Pentagon documents, reported the figure as 560. He didn't include, because it didn't include, the 400 in Afghanistan. The best estimates are between 1,000 and 1,200, but it is indeed difficult to keep track. Ask (as you begin to trade your dollars for yuan) how many our feared rival, lender in chief, and now owner of the No. 2 economy in the world China has: the answer is zero.

The never-ending Afghan War provides, win, lose, or stalemate, never-ending riches for our former generals' new firms. Meanwhile, our continuous droning of suspected militants in the nearby tribal areas of Pakistan, which kills untold civilians, is making extremism and radicalism intensify, as that nuclear-armed nation creeps closer to chaos. The very worst thing that could happen for us — fanatical Islamists in control of The Bomb — is precisely the course our CIA and DoD geniuses are taking us toward.

Where is the "free" media in all this madness? The MIC of Ike's day is now MIC MAC. For an explanation see Condor's next column....

-January 17, 2011

---

*   Devoted reader and advisor Wayne County (MI) Circuit Judge David
     Allen holds the distinction of having escaped the Truman Show
     before Condor.

Chapter Twenty-three

Sycophants Supreme

> *"No nation can preserve its freedom in the midst of perpetual warfare."*
>
> – James Madison

The Wall Street Journal, America's best charmingly neo-fascist media source, reported February 17 that former Soviet Union Premier Mikhail Gorbachev had recently blasted the current Russian regime for, among other faults, "eroding the free media." He opined that the ongoing Egyptian revolt could likely happen in Russia but "in an even more staggering way."

There is no chance of such erosion by government intervention happening in the United States. Here, the "free" media has eroded itself, by latching onto, in the most subservient manner, the military-industrial-congressional complex. The sycophantic Elite Eight are as follows: Disney/ABC, Comcast-GE/NBC, National Amusements/CBS, Time Warner/CNN, *The New York Times*, *The Washington Post*, and our banksters' beloved News Corp (Fox TV and, for its select literate viewers, the aforementioned WSJ).

The Elite Eight are all part of mammoth corporations; the stated goal of each is to earn as large a profit as possible. The most efficient way to increase profit is, of course, to avoid in any way possible paying one's fair share of taxes. So, like their fellow large corporate brethren, the Elite Eight's owners devise all manner of schemes so that individual Americans (excepting the richest 1 percent) can shoulder ever more of the overall tax burden. Better yet, the extra cash saved by tax avoidance allows them to employ attractive courtiers to explain to the rest of us why we need to accept less while paying more. These courtiers — nearly everyone you see on TV — serve the Washington echo chamber extremely well and, by never asking serious questions, are handsomely rewarded with fame, grotesque salaries, and continued access to those in power.

Consider NBC parent General Electric. *The New York Times* reported that GE had paid 14.3 percent in taxes from 2005 - 2009, far below the 35 percent it is supposed to pay. But it turns out GE actually only paid 3.4% over that period. Also, it received a $74 billion guaranty of its debt by lobbying the Feds to broaden a bailout program initially used for banks in the Great Giveaway of 2008-09. The kicker? Chief Welfare Recipient Jeffrey Immelt, GE's CEO, now heads President Obama's economic advisory panel. So recovery (its, not ours) is practically assured.

In the run-up to the Iraq War, when any journalist speaking the truth about Saddam Hussein's non-existent WMDs was frozen from the Elite Eight, the Eighters and abettors championed White House war propaganda, headlined false stories, kept Americans in a state of constant fear and confusion, and led more than 80 percent of our citizens to wrongly believe Iraq had assisted the 9/11 attacks.

Today, no better example of corporatized media's true sympathies can be found than in the *Post* and the *Times* (commonly referred to as "liberal" papers in the winningest propaganda of our day) rejecting not one, but five consecutive op-ed pieces submitted by former Army colonel and current professor Andrew Bacevich, the leading anti-imperial voice we currently possess. Conversely, completely discredited neocon apparatchik John "Nuts and" Bolton's columns have appeared during that span no fewer than four times in the *Post* and thrice more in the *Times*.

Another *Times* tidbit concerns the travails of Raymond Davis, the CIA contractor-operative who has been arrested for killing two people in Pakistan. These deaths have merely threatened diplomatic relations between the U.S. and its mutually distrusted ally. The Pakistanis believed (correctly, it turns out) Davis had been working for Xe, the private security firm which changed its name from Blackwater to help people from reflexively thinking "Thugs, Incorporated."

Though the Obama administration initially denied Davis was anything other than a diplomat, it now admits that he is, in fact, a CIA contractor. What's amazing here is that the *Times* now states that it knew all along about Davis's role, but continued to keep mum at the Administration's request. Only when Britain's *The Guardian* reported that the *Times* and other media outlets were "checking" with the U.S. government to learn what it could and what it could not report, did the Obamaites release the truth. As Glenn Greenwald noted in Salon, "That's called being an active enabler of government propaganda."

And on February 22 our unofficial "Newspaper of Record" published an op-ed cheering on the Afghan War with this gem, "It now seems more likely than not that the country can achieve the modest level of stability and self-reliance necessary to allow the U.S. to responsibly draw down their forces from 100,000 to 25,000 troops over the next four years." Let's see, that brings us to 2015, and then we're still there, just with "only" 25,000 troops . . .

But *The Times* is proud of its distributor role. In its seventy editorials regarding Iraq from 9/11 to the March 2003 invasion the phrases "UN Charter" and "international law" never appeared. Why? Because *The Times* agreed completely with the Bush/Cheney Junta's War of Choice.

As our democracy slides closer to oblivion, nicely exemplified by the Army's reported illegal use of psychological tactics (psy-ops) to manipulate U.S. senators to continue supporting the Afghan Inferno, let us not forget the magnificent part the Elite Eight have played. The final piece of the MICMAC puzzle (Military-Industrial-Congressional-Media-?-Complex) shall be revealed next column.

-February 2011

War Kickoff Weekend

Spectacularly coinciding with college football's opening game on ESPN, the MICMAC (Military-Industrial-Congressional-Media-Academic Complex) Cougars began their 64th season since the start of the Korean War last Thursday with typical fanfare and excitement. This year's season opener vs. Syria was hoped by neocon schedule makers to lead to a long awaited bowl showdown later with Iran. As always, the mandated "play-in" game against the perennially pathetic Constitutional Condors was allowed and, like Michigan vs. CMU, promised an easy romp for the Cougars so that the real season could get underway.

Head coach Martin Dempsey (Chairman Joint Chiefs of Staff), though normally as pessimistic as Frank Leahy was during Notre Dame's glory years, has such an explosive attack that he's even letting fifth year quarterback Barry "Choom" Obama call some of his own plays. Odds makers installed MICMAC as four touchdown favorites over the Condors, whose weak defense consists only of truth, reason, and (for now) the American public, whom polls indicate are against a Syrian War-perhaps partly because 1) no self-defense of the U.S. being involved, and 2) no UN Security Council resolution makes any attack of Syria blatantly illegal under international law.

Undeterred by the fact that striking the Syrian regime would de- facto help the opposition, who happen to include al-Qaeda and its allies, MICMAC started the game on Thursday with a media blitz led by Obama's safe passes to wide receivers Judy Woodruff and Gwen Ifill of PBS. The Cougars' first series of downs featured the QB saying, "When countries break international norms on weapons like chemical weapons that could threaten us, they are held accountable." Consulting with allies was made paramount, team officials stated.

Unfortunately, late in the quarter All-American flanker David "The Poodle" Cameron (British Prime Minister), ready to help execute Obama's plays, was viciously chop-blocked from the sidelines by his own Parliament (a 285-273 No War vote) and was rendered incapacitated for the rest of the game, a stunning blow for all Cougar fans. The Condors ended the first quarter trailing but for once not downhearted.

The second quarter (Friday) saw QB Obama hand the ball off to star tailback John Kerry (Secretary of State). Kerry gave a powerful open field address zigzagging around Constitutional defenders, stating that the U.S. has "high confidence" that Syria's government was responsible for the August 21 chemical weapons attack outside Damascus and history would judge us "extraordinarily harshly if we turned a blind eye" to the atrocity. It was such a performance that leading MICMAC cheerleader *The Washington Post* headlined "John Kerry makes a forceful case for U.S. Military Intervention in Syria," naturally leaving out of its story any voice opposed to that of its team.

Naturally, too, no MICMAC media outlet dared mention an explosive August 26 *Foreign Policy* story which used top-secret CIA memos from the 1980s to show that not only did the U.S. know that Saddam Hussein's Iraq used chemical weapons against Iran, killing far more than were slaughtered in Syria on August 21, but that we actively supported Iraq and covered up its CW use so no international outcry would ensue. But play-by-play announcers on Fox, CNN et al passed on revealing this information, since it might incite normally supportive Cougar fans to begin openly rooting for the Condors.

The third quarter (Saturday) opening drive featured a trick play-QB Obama punted on *second* down to Congress, in a move not seen in Washington since the days of FDR and the single wing formation. A perfectly timed 1:50pm speech (allowing Michigan and Notre Dame fans to settle in for their respective 3:30pm kickoffs) had Obama welcome a Congressional vote the week of September 9 on the matter, cleverly leaving in his "Secret Option Play"-where he could strike Syria even if Congress voted against it. This left media cheerleaders and the war establishment confused, but the QB had seen polls showing 79% of fans wanted congressional authorization or, in other words, the Supreme Law of the Land to be actually observed.

The fourth quarter (Sunday), like the first three did not allow the Condors the ball (so they couldn't actually make their case in corporate media), but Kerry ran five consecutive halfback option plays (MICMAC doesn't follow four down rules like other teams; it simply keeps the ball until it scores) on *Fox News Sunday*, NBC's *Meet the Press*, ABC's *This Week*, CBS's *Face the Nation*, and CNN's *State of the Union*. In this instance, Kerry chose to throw deep desperation passes that landed incomplete on all five networks, and his cause wasn't helped when, helmetless, he was made to look by his make-up artist like Boris Karloff in *The Mummy*.

At regulation's end the game was, incredibly, still tied, thereby requiring an unprecedented overtime period. Quarterback and coach may have to huddle with the MICMAC Board of Directors itself (stuffed as it is with representatives from the major defense contractors and Wall Street megabanks) to ensure Congressional skeptics don't threaten the squad with internal dissension. Don't bet against the intervention but, for now, be aware that just getting into OT has lifted the spirits of the longtime winless Constitutional Condors, heretofore the Chicago Cubs of Warfare Football.

-September 2013

Chapter Twenty-four

Quintet

> "The President does not have the power under the Constitution to unilaterally authorize a military attack in a situation that does not involve stopping an actual or imminent threat to the nation."
>
> –Harvard Law Graduate and Constitutional Law Professor **Barack Obama,** 2007

Two decades after the University of Michigan's Fab Five hoopsters began their arresting run at winning nothing, and one since the U.S. Supreme Court's version (starring one Yale, one Stanford, and three Harvard educated jurists) appointed as president the loser of the 2000 election, the national wreckage from one of these two heralded quintets has clearly emerged. It is therefore time to pay homage to the last and most celebrated pillar of a different pentagonal entity—The Military-Industrial-Congressional-Media-Academic Complex (MICMAC): American Academia.

Though my siblings' beloved U-M, along with Condor's own MSU, are part of the Financial 50—the fifty universities with endowments of at least $1 billion—our two state Public Ivies pale in alumni power and influence compared to the central Fab Five of this piece: Harvard (with a $27.6 billion endowment), Yale ($16.7), Princeton ($14.4), Stanford ($13.7), and MIT ($8.3). MIT at first glance appears to be Phillip Tattaglia to Harvard's Vito Corleone, but the science-centered institution can boast of being No. 1 in Department of Defense awarded research, to the tune of more than $600 million annually.

MIT is hardly alone. More than 350 civilian colleges and universities, conduct Pentagon-funded research. Financial 50's Harvard, Columbia, Cal-Berkeley, and Johns Hopkins each receive in excess of $100 million every NCAA basketball season. In fact, the DoD is third in overall funding to U.S. civilian universities, behind only the National Institute of Health and National Science Foundation. And in this era of dwindling budget revenues, the Pentagon's clout allows it to dictate just what type of research it wants done. So much for the idea of independent higher education.

Of course, this does not even factor in the more than 150 exclusively military schools now funded by Joey and Josie Taxpayer. The National War College, School for National Security Executive Education, Defense Acquisition University, and Marine Corps University may not yet be recruiting quarterbacks from Birmingham Brother Rice like brethren Army, Navy, and Air Force. However, with "only" 778 college football games televised in 2011, many with military sponsorship, there's an obvious growth market in competing for fans' attention spans.

Returning to those schools most richly endowed, what is their true purpose? "To perpetuate their own," argues (Harvard educated) journalist Chris Hedges. These institutions do a superb job turning out competent systems managers, the main system's components being that 1) The Market is self-regulating, and 2) the U.S. must police the world, for the good of all. Questioning the system itself is never an option. Questioning its components leaves one a pariah, an outsider, a Ralph Nader. Question the system and one becomes, in the MICMAC structure, a nonperson.

Superb examples of MICMAC's self-sustenance can be offered by two additional Fab Fives. The previous administration gave us, in (perhaps) reverse seeding importance:

5. **Condi Rice** (Stanford Professor), the National Security Advisor who testified she forgot, then ignored, repeated urgent warnings from underlings about al-Qaeda's threat inside the U.S. in summer 2001. She was later made Secretary of State.

4. **Chris Cox** (Harvard MBA, JD), the SEC head who allowed investment banks in 2004 to go from traditional

10-1 leverage lending to a calamitous 30-1 because, well, the chief of Goldman Sachs asked him to.

3. **Donald Rumsfeld** (Princeton), the Secretary of Defense genius who, inspired by Milton Friedman's Chicago School of Economics theories, privatized the Pentagon so that we may now pay $1 million per soldier, per year, in Afghanistan, mainly to multinational corporations who avoid paying U.S. taxes.

2. **Henry Paulsen,** (Dartmouth), the Treasury Secretary who first denied, then be(Elmer)fuddledly presided over the U.S. Megabank collapse four years after asking Cox for 30-1 leverage—Yes, folks, it was Hanky who was the Goldman Sachs' CEO referred to above.

1. **George W. Bush** (Yale, Harvard MBA), who was described by his first Treasury Secretary Paul O'Neill at cabinet meetings as "The blind man in a room of deaf ears," arguably the most accurate accounting offered in American political annals.

The current one, apparently attempting to do the previously unthinkable—outdo the Bush Team in cluelessness—bequeaths us:

5 **Lawrence Summers** (Harvard, MIT), the Clinton administration's champion of derivatives' non-regulation and repeal of Glass-Steagall who, for his lack of common sense, was recycled by Obama and named National Economic Council Director.

4. **Timothy Geithner** (Dartmouth), New York Federal Reserve head who steered $62 billion to reckless banks to save even more reckless insurer AIG from its huge

losses, then told AIG to "keep quiet" about the taxpayer gift in SEC filings. As punishment, Obama named him Treasury Secretary.

3. **Ben Bernanke** (Harvard, MIT), hapless Federal Reserve Chairman appointed by Bush, but reappointed by Obama after proving to the world that Wall Street looters must be rewarded at the expense of forgiving taxpayers.

2. **Hillary Clinton** (Yale JD), the de-facto President for Foreign Policy, who finds no bad brutal dictator too unimportant for us to attack, and no good brutal dictator (good defined as "one who does what we want") too offensive to defend.

1. **Barack Obama** (Harvard JD), who, in perhaps our most surreal political moment yet, briefly interrupted his NCAA bracket picks to announce his unconstitutional bombing of Libya. He did, to be fair, quickly return to hoops analysis, reassuring all the priorities of his first term.

Hedges ominously warned, in early 2009, not to expect the power elites to save us. "They don't know how. They don't even know how to ask the questions."

And as the Fab Five Supremes, Universities, Bushies, Obamaites, and MICMAC itself demonstrate, the power elite do not even adhere to laws like the rest of us do. Because of these factors, they've given the foes of the American Republic a sizeable lead, and it is probably late in the fourth quarter. We the People can only hope to somehow rally and, when a needed time out is called, pray we, unlike Chris Webber, actually have one left.

-March 2011

Five Reasons to Bomb Syria

Thirty months after "Quintet," it is clear the foes of the American Republic indeed maintain a large lead, but they may be starting to squander it. U.S. corporate media, despite herculean efforts to support an attack on Syria, is reluctantly reporting that the U.S. House of Representatives will likely defeat a proposed war resolution. This scenario sets up a potential constitutional crisis as President Barack Obama, channeling his Choom Gang leadership days in Hawaii, has more than hinted he might well bomb the devastated war-torn Middle East nation anyway.

"The stupidest war in western history," preemptively writes seven-time British International Journalist of the Year recipient Robert Fisk. Why on earth would the U.S. government, in the face of overwhelming domestic public opposition and little international support, intervene in such a foolish manner?

In defense of the White House Choomsters, Condor lists five reasons:

1. **IF AT FIRST YOU DON'T SUCCEED** - for over 30 years now, the U.S. has many times blundered militarily into the Greater Middle East - none of which have led to objectives being achieved. From Beirut in 1982-83 to Iraq (Madeline Albright, later to be named Secretary of State, infamously admitted on CBS's *60 Minutes* "We think the price is worth it" when asked about the reported 500,000 deaths of Iraqi children caused by U.S. sanctions against that nation), to Somalia, to drone strikes in Pakistan,

Afghanistan, and Yemen, to bombing in Libya - all have led to greater hatred and distrust of the U.S. - and not quelled unrest in these countries, so add Syria to the list of mindless foreign policy moves - consistency is our greatest virtue.

2. **STICK BY OLD FRIENDS** - The House of Saud, that loveable regime whose country gave us 15 of the 19 September 11th terrorists, has its former U.S. Ambassador back in action. Remember Bandar bin Sultan, who was so chummy with a certain American political family that he was known as Bandar Bush? He's the man who made a cool $2 billion (*while* Ambassador) in an $80 billion British-to-Saudi arms deal; Tony Blair's attorney general stopped bin Sultan's fraud investigation in midstream because it would have led to "the complete wreckage of a vital strategic relationship and the loss of thousands of British jobs."

    Well, Bandar is back - as Director of Saudi Intelligence, and is leading the Saudi funneling of arms to the Syrian rebels. It has been reported he is head moneyman of John Kerry's Arsenal of Arabs willing to underwrite the U.S. attack. What could be better for the empty coffers of the U.S. Treasury? Our military contractors get paid by Saud & Friends to make their munitions, and if war causes the price of oil to spike, who cares if American drivers pay an extra 50¢ per gallon of gas? It's a win/win for MICMAC and Saudi oil profits.

3. **KEEP THE STREAK ALIVE** - The most powerful lobby in foreign affairs, dwarfing all competitors, is AIPAC (The American Israel Public Affairs Committee). Though most Americans aren't even aware of its existence, in the last three decades The Lobby has become so effective that

openly defying its wishes is tantamount to ending one's hope for career advancement in Washington or, in some cases, ending one's career itself (see the political corpses of Charles Percy, Paul Findley, and Charles Freeman). Israel's newspaper *Haaretz* (which, unlike U.S. media, doesn't censor mention of AIPAC's immense clout) admitted on September 6 that not since 1991 has a major Lobby initiative been defeated. And *Politico* reported two days prior that 250 AIPAC members and allies were set to "storm the halls of Congress" to pass Obama's resolution. So with Congress getting its ears blistered by angry constituents fed up with perpetual war, one has to root for the underdog (in this contest)...The ($$) Green AIPACkers.

4. **ADVANCE "DEMOCRACY"** - Another of our friends in our stated quest for promoting democracy is Sheikh Hamad bin Khalifa Al-Thani, the former Emir of Qatar, who ruled the not-quite-democratic Muslim monarchy from 1995 to this past June, when he handed off leadership duties in the World's Richest County (per capita income) to his 33 year old son (control of Qatar has been part of the family portfolio since the 19th century).

In addition to being the largest property holder in London, Qatar's sovereign Investment Authority has purchased Harrod's, 12.6% of Barclay's, 75% of Miramax Films, a French soccer team, and is in talks to buy Neiman Marcus. And Qatar started and owns that U..S. right wingers' go-to-source for news - *Al Jazeera*.

Qatar has also spent freely on arming the Syrian rebels, to a reported tune of $3 billion. A liquefied natural gas pipeline to Europe through Syria would make the World's Wealthiest even wealthier though, and cut into the Russian company Gazprom's energy supplying dominance to the European market. Getting rid of Bashar al-Assad (a Shi'i) and replacing him with fellow Sunnis (the rebels) is a nice bonus.

5. **PROTECT THE VULNERABLE** - On September 5, *The New York Times, ProPublica,* and *The Guardian* published the latest Edward Snowden revelations regarding the National Security Agency - perhaps the most damaging yet. It was reported that the NSA is, literally, a saboteur of encryption systems - so that anything online supposedly secure for *any of us* - banking transactions, medical records, communications, has been deliberately weakened by the NSA. This makes it easier for hackers to unscramble data they steal. The NSA did this, ostensibly, to disrupt encryptions of "terrorists." But the agency itself can now get inside anyone's privacy records.

The abuse goes beyond its earlier reported (illegal but mere) monitoring of Americans' private communications. But with the "Crisis in Syria" dominating corporate news, maybe the NSA, now presumably vulnerable to the ire of Americans who value privacy and safety from theft, can dodge the total wrath of a distracted populace.

So on behalf of the House of Saud, AIPAC, Qatar's Emirs (father and son), the NSA, and all those ill-advising military interventionists since the christening of the Carter Doctrine, the Syrian Attack Supporters SALUTE YOU TEAM OBAMA!

-September 2013

Chapter Twenty-five

Safe Harbor

The following is the printed text of Condor's remarks made before the Detroit Catholic Central Shamrock Bar Association on April 12, 2011.

Good evening! I have no idea why I am up here, except that word has perhaps gotten out of what I always tell alumni of Brother Rice, De La Salle, and "That Vile Seven Mile Institution,"* — two years at Catholic Central are worth more than four years anyplace else (applause). I normally also tell people that I studied more hours in two years at CC than in three years at Cooley but, with Justice Brennan in attendance, I'll forgo that line tonight. You know, when I started at Cooley the only attorney I even knew was my cousin Ed Plawecki, who advised me not to go to law school because "There are already too many lawyers." That was in 1984. I wonder if I can get a response from the founder of a school that in 2010 had 3,664 students (Note: apparently anticipating Condor's remarks, Justice Brennan was a no-show for his Distinguished Lawyer Award).

I write a column called "Confessions of a Condor", and let me start with three confessions: 1) I left CC in 1977 because of a slight disagreement between the Basilian Fathers' dominions and me over my athletic abilities — they didn't think I had any. So I took my well-disguised talents to the Dearborn Heights Riverside Rebels, where I played tennis and was the shooting guard on arguably the best 2-17 basketball squad in state history. 2) I did NOT then put a curse on the CC basketball team, saying they'd never reach the state semis again (11 times previously achieved), although the record shows that is exactly what has transpired since I left — despite some outstanding teams, some very controversial calls and no-calls in 1996, 1998, 2002, and just last month have prevented the boys from advancing. Nevertheless, I fully expect the 2012 edition to break the three-and-a-half decade drought.** 3) I WAS the first to say that the primary reason the school moved to Novi was so that the hoopsters could finally win a regional title, and one was brought home, after 26 years in the wilderness, in 2009.

My column began as "Spartacus." I wrote my first in late 2000 in response to a column called "From the Right" by a Michigan Court of Appeals judge which argued that the Florida Supreme Court had messed up things so badly in the Bush-Gore recount that the U.S. Supremes, despite there being no Federal issue in the case, had to intervene. The idea of Spartacus, who led a slave uprising against ancient Rome, was that I'd be writing "from below," since as a district judge I knew I could be overruled by a higher court.

I then basically took four years off to write a book about major league pitchers which argued, among other things, that a formula I had created did indeed prove that Judge Roland Olzark's teammate Art Houtteman was the best American League pitcher of 1950, and also that Frank Tanana was, with one exception, the best 22- and 23-year-old pitcher in MLB history. Why did I do this? As former Circuit Judge Richard Hathaway once said, "District judges have way too much time on their hands."

I've since changed the name [of the column] to "Confessions of a Condor" — as in California Condor (CC again), a rare bird that lives mainly in captivity (much like a judge with three teen-age daughters) and is from the family *falconiformes* (my three are Divine Child Falcons). Condors are vultures who feast on dead animals, much as I feast on and borrow the ideas of great minds in history and tradition, which Chesterton calls "a democracy of the dead." "Confessions" I stole from my favorite book, Garry Wills' "Confessions of a Conservative." Wills in turn had been inspired by his favorite thinker — Saint Augustine, who, at the end of the 4th century, wrote his own "Confessions." "Confessions" in this literature means not only an admission of guilt, but also a profession of faith.

So what do I, hopefully without pontificating, profess tonight? Briefly, the underpinnings of American elite educational institutions have been girded by two constant ideas: 1) The Market is rational and self-regulating, and 2) the U.S. must police the world, for the good of all.

The first idea has been spectacularly shredded to smithereens with the financial meltdown of 2007-09. This was caused mainly by 1) the repeal of Glass-Steagall, which removed the previously existing separation between Wall Street investment banks and commercial banks, 2) the non-regulation of derivatives, and 3) allowing banks' leverage to go from 10-1 to 30-1. Light regulation is, says Robert Shiller, "one of the most remarkable errors in the history of thought."

The second is very much alive and revered by the elite. It had a more sound basis than pillar one — The Cold War. We were locked in a Manichean struggle with the godless Soviet Union, "A third world country with a first world military," CC's legendary history teacher Frank Garlicki told us lower classmen that "we will, in our lifetimes, see collapse."

The Gar was right! The Cold War ended-with us as lone superpower. But in the two decades since, our military has become ever more bloated, ever more wasteful, ever more controlling of our civic affairs. An unaccounted for $2.3 *trillion* in the Pentagon, our Defense Secretary told us on 9/10/01. But that was forgotten a day later...

Seven hundred billion spent last year — which doesn't include veterans' benefits and medical care, storage of nuclear weapons, State Department foreign aid, interest on the debt from past wars, the CIA, the NSA, or Homeland Security. Meanwhile, the U.S. infrastructure of roads, bridges, sewers, airports, trains, and mass transit are in dismal disrepair. Our empire of over 1,000 foreign bases, unknown to most Americans, is unsustainable. Now *we* are on the verge of becoming the Third World Country with a First World Military.

So, I say: End the Empire! Restore the Republic! Stop electing Harvard, Yale, Princeton, and Stanford types.***

"Teach me Goodness, Discipline, and Knowledge,"

And get some CC alumni in the nation's leadership — as long as they remember that of the Basilian Trinitarian school motto "Teach me Goodness, Discipline, and Knowledge," Goodness comes first. For without Goodness, Discipline and Knowledge lead nowhere. Thank you.

-April 2011

---

*   University of Detroit Jesuit High School, perhaps CC's main rival in academic excellence.

**   It didn't.

***   Excepting *falconiformes*-eldest daughter Rachel is currently studying at Yale.

21 Gun Salute

For many years Condor has carried a PocketPal calendar. In the back of the calendar* are a few blank pages for notes of advance planning. Every year sees a new quote or two jotted down, and recopied old quotes into subsequent year's additions. My 21 quotes from PocketPal 2013, in nearly random order:

1. *All members shall refrain in their international relations from the threat or use of force against the territorial integrity or political independence of any state.*

   -UN Charter Article II (4)

No mention of this bedrock principle of international law ever creeps into MICMAC media's reporting when the U.S. threatens another sovereign country. See the "Crisis in Syria" for the latest example.

2. *The Spirit has been incorporated, but the process has failed.*

   -Rene Girard

Girard's interpretation of why violence threatens humanity's existence despite Christians' belief of the presence of the Holy Spirit is the most provocative writing of our time.

3. *War is nothing but a dual on a larger scale.*

   -Clausewitz

Football is war on a (slightly) more gentle basis. Hence its immense popularity-particularly in the South.

4. *If tyranny and oppression come to this land, it will be in the guise of fighting a foreign enemy.*

   -James Madison

5. *No nation could preserve its freedom in the midst of continual warfare.*

   -Madison again

Twelve years and counting since 9/11- the truth of Madison's maxims is seen everyday. No purses allowed at Michigan State University football games, Condor's wife learned upon attempting entry to Spartan Stadium in September 2013. Courtesy the Department of Homeland Security, the right and left wings (Military and Academic) of MICMAC working in perfect tandem once again.

6. *Wars are occasioned by the love of money.*

   -Socrates

One of the Wise Man's curiously lesser reported nuggets.

7. *Too much capitalism does not mean too many capitalists, but too few capitalists.*

   -GK Chesterton

Chesterton's list of witty and insightful quotes is as large as the man was himself.

8. *Nonetheless, some of us entertain a fondness for the quaint old Constitution. It may be too late to return to its ideals, but the effort should be made.*

As Cyrano said, "One fights not only in the hope of winning."
                                        -Garry Wills

Those words inspired Condor to seriously consider running for Congress in 2010. However, cowardice and/or common sense eventually negated a potential race against GOP stalwart Thaddeus "Invalid Signatures" McCotter.

9   *When there's a Republican president I'm a Democrat.*
     When there's a Democratic president I'm out of step.
                                        -T.P. Gore

Condor's spiritual ancestor.

10. *Some things are under our control. Some things are not.*
                                        -Epictetus

Something that bears daily repeating.

11. *Near is,*
    And difficult to grasp, the God.
    But where danger threatens
    That which saves from it also
    grows.
                                        -Friedrich Holderlin

Rene Girard has interpreted this German poet's works and descent into "madness" to reveal the escalating crisis of humanity. See Girard's *Battling to the End* for further explanation.

12. *The built in restlessness of human incompleteness*
    is channeled into the will to consume and acquire,

> *which fuels the illusion that the restlessness can be*
> *quieted by satisfaction of the next desire.*
>
> **-James Carroll**

Mad Men, arguably the best series in television history, nicely exemplifies this Carrollian observation.

> 13. *The nationalist not only does not disapprove of*
> *the atrocities committed by his own side, but he*
> *has a remarkable capacity for not even hearing*
> *about them.*
>
> **-George Orwell**

In May 2013 former Guatemala dictator Efrain Rios Montt was convicted of genocide against his own people for his regime's actions from the early 1980s. The Reagan Administration assisted Montt militarily during his entire reign of terror. President Reagan at the time said Montt was getting "a bum rap" from human rights groups

Most American nationalists lionize Mr. Reagan's legacy. MICMAC media assists them by keeping silent on U.S. complicity in such endeavors.

> 14. *Remember particularly that you cannot be a judge*
> *of anyone. For no one can judge a criminal until he*
> *recognizes that he is just such a criminal as the man*
> *standing before him, and that he perhaps is more*
> *than all men to blame for that crime.*
>
> **-Dostoevsky, The Brothers Karamazov**

> 15. *Loving with human love, one may change from love*
> *to hatred; but divine love cannot change. Nothing,*
> *not even death, can shatter it. It is the very nature of*
> *the soul.*
>
> **-Tolstoy, War and Peace**

Along with Shakespeare, these two 19th century Russian writers represent the highest rendering of the combined understanding and portrayal of the human condition. J.M. Coetzee's tribute to them in *Diary of a Bad Year* is precisely accurate.

16. *I agree to this Constitution, with all its faults, if they are such: because I think a General Government necessary for us, and there is no form of Government but what may be a Blessing to the People if well administered; and I believe farther that this is likely to be well administered for a Course of Years, and can only end in Despotism as other forms have done before it, when the People shall become so corrupted as to need Despotic Government, being incapable of any other.*
    -Benjamin Franklin, September 17, 1787

At least one founder saw it all quite clearly.

17. *I disclaim all patriotism incompatible with the principles of eternal justice.*
    -John Quincy Adams

America has never been as full of patriots as she is now.

18. *All civilization is centralization. All centralization is economy. Under economical centralization, Asia is cheaper than Europe. The world tends toward economic centralization. Therefore, Asia tends to survive and Europe to perish.*
    -Brooks Adams

Our long-term "engagement" in Vietnam explained, circa 1910.

19. *A continually expanding subsystem of a finite system carries within the seeds of its own demise. An ever expanding economy divided by a finite planet does not compute.*

-Tim Jackson.

This would appear to be simple math. Appearances appear to be deceiving the leaders of the world.

20. *The U.S. government exists primarily to make the world safe for multinational corporations, but those firms feel no obligation to pay for that protection in return.*

-Robert Scheer

If Scheer's first statement is true, then the U.S. government has been unfairly maligned, particularly by Condor. It is doing a *superb* job of protecting multinationals (at the expense of everyone else).

21. *Civilization is a thing of the calm, the patient, the pragmatic, and the wise. We are not assured that it will triumph.*

-James J. O'Donnell

I would observe that, in late 2013, we are nearly assured that civilization will *not* triumph, but I prefer to give the late antiquity scholar and *Ruin of the Roman Empire* author the last (and less pessimistic) word.

---

*   Courtesy top-notch Detroit area attorney and former Purdue University catcher Steven Bullock.

Chapter Twenty-Six

Yes Chipster, there is a Climate Claus

On April 6, the GOP House defeated, by a 240-184 margin, Democratic Congressman Henry Waxman's amendment to a bill stating, "Congress accepts the scientific findings of the Environmental Protection Agency that climate change is occurring, is caused largely by human activities, and poses significant risks for public health and welfare."

The proposed resolution's language was taken almost verbatim from that adopted by the U.S. National Academy of Sciences. NAS, created by legislation signed by President Abraham Lincoln in 1863, is an organization whose 2,100 members include nearly 200 Nobel Prize winners, a sort of Hall of Fame for the highest achieving living individuals of their fields. It is one of 32 national academies in the world, from Canada to Great Britain to Germany to China to Australia, that has gone on record supporting the United Nations' Intergovernmental Panel on Climate Change (IPCC) 2007 assessment that global warming is unequivocally real, very likely (meaning a 90 to 99 percent probability) due to man, and a threat to civilization. The number of science academies neutral to or opposing the assessment: zero.

Since then, Condor received a query (of sorts) from good friend and conscientious attorney Chip Kleinbrook, worried (still) about liberal institutions like science academies and their nefarious plot to alarm people. I paraphrase:

DEAR CONDOR:

I was very recently (forty) nine years old. Some (all) of my liberal friends say there is no Climate Claus. The most extreme of them say, "If you see it in Condor it's so." Please tell me the truth; is there a Climate Claus?

Chip Kleinbrook
Tea Party Enthusiast

CONDOR'S RESPONSE:

Chipster, your little-faithed friends are wrong. They have been affected by the unfortunate use of physics and chemistry. They think that nothing can be which is not comprehensible by their Maddow-infested minds.

Yes, Chipster, there is a Climate Claus. He exists as certainly as do the cerebellums of Limbaugh and O'Reilly. Alas! How dreary would life be if there was no Climate Claus. It would be as dreary as if there were no Chipsters. When you and your friends see that 2010 was the warmest year on record (that means since 1880), and that 12 of the 14 warmest years have happened since 1997, and that 2010 was also the wettest year on record (wait 'til this year's data are compiled), and that Pakistan's July flood covered an unprecedented 20 percent of the country, and that Russia's warmest summer ever caused record wildfires, and that Australia in December and January suffered its worst flooding ever, and that Texas wildfires this year alone have burned over 2.5 million acres and its drought is worse than the 1930s Dust Bowl, and that the Amazon rainforest experienced its second "once in a century" drought in five years, and that the accelerating rate of decline in Arctic ice continues, which will in turn melt the permafrost, release frozen methane, and thus greatly increase warming further yet, well, Climate Claus understands why your faith may be a bit shaken.

Troubling, too, is that the IPCC, which received input from nearly every important climatologist on earth, predicted more then a decade ago that because warm air holds more water vapor than does cold, evaporation in dry areas and deluge in wet ones (rain and snow) will increase; in other words, precisely what has been taking place across the globe. Climate Claus feels your angst.

But fear not, Chip! Climate Claus, who admittedly gives us these periodic unsettling events can, when he so chooses, magically isolate from each other all of the aforementioned occurrences, and thus return peace of mind and climate tranquility to those who, say, wonder why this April saw more tornados than any in U.S. history, or why the Mississippi is flooding like it hasn't since the year Babe Ruth hit 60 Yankee homers.

Also, with the help of the unbiased media, which reports all the mounting (and mountainous) evidence of global warming with "not so fast" responses from fossil fuel industry funded institutes, we can keep folks as well informed as we did during the Oswald Acted Alone, Smoking Causes Cancer, and Man Went to the Moon frauds.

Not believe in Climate Claus? You might as well not believe in Sean Hannity! Did you ever see Sean breakdancing on your lawn? Of course not, but that's no proof he's not there.

You may tear apart Glen Beck's rattle and see what makes the noise inside (Glen: "Bill McKibben's 350.org is a communist conspiracy"), but there is a veil covering the unseen world which no one can tear apart. Is it real? Ah, Chipster, there is nothing else real and abiding like Senator Inhofe's belief that "the threat of catastrophic global warming is the greatest hoax ever perpetrated on the American people."

No Climate Clause? Thank (our rightwing) God he lives, and he lives forever. A year from now, Chip, nay, ten times ten years from now, he will, with the Koch brothers' billions and their descendants' minimally taxed trust funds, continue to make glad, and of course, warm, the heart of the political party in America that has chosen to deny reality.

-June 2011

Five Minutes to Midnight

World Overshoot Day, aka Ecological Debt Day, is the date each year when what humanity collectively consumes in earthly resources exceeds the planet's capacity for that year's regeneration. Throughout human history, the earth's capacity was greater than what man could extract from the ground, produce from the land, and emit into the air. With rapidly increasing population and industrial development, by the 1970s man's consumption began to outstrip what the earth could replenish. World Overshoot Day in 1987 happened on December 19 and in 1995 on November 21. By 2005, it had moved up to October 20.

In 2013, Ecological Debt Day arrived on August 20, its earliest date yet. We are now using the equivalent of 1.5 earths each year to sustain our global way of life. In the United States, we use the equivalent of four earths. This trend is obviously not sustainable, and is causing havoc that is becoming more and more noticeable to even the most isolated of Chipster's friends in the Truman Show.

Boulder, Colorado in September 2013 received more rainfall in a three day period (12.30") than it had ever received in a previous month (9.59" in May 1995). MICMAC media predictably covered this horrific event, which killed at least seven in Colorado and destroyed an estimated 1900 homes, with its usual silent treatment-let's-connect-no-dots-non-mention of climate change. This despite the chilling report from the National Weather Center itself: "MAJOR FLOODING/FLASH FLOODING EVENT UNDERWAY AT THIS TIME WITH BIBLICAL RAINFALL AMOUNTS REPORTED IN MANY AREAS…"

Yes, "Biblical" was used-a nice touch for interested creationists. According to the pre-eminent *Weather Underground* site, it was a greater than 1-in-1000 rainfall event. Republican meteorologist Paul Douglas, an outlier in the "I see nothing, I know nothing" party of Sgt. Schultzes, commented that since the record Arctic ice melt of 2012, he has seen that "the jet stream has been misbehaving; more blocking patterns in general over the northern hemisphere." A weakening of the jet stream causes more fixed weather patterns. The same "blocking" atmospheric flow pattern caused Calgary's $5.3 billion flood in June, the most expensive in Canadian history.

The Colorado deluge comes on the heels of massive wildfires seen throughout the state in June and July 2013, which were a virtual replay of the record wildfires in summer 2012. Almost contemporaneous were the California wildfires near Yosemite National Park which, optimistic Chipsters can chirp, was only the *fourth* largest blaze (370 square miles) in the Golden State's recorded annals. Record temperatures played a part in all these events, to the surprise of no climatologist not funded by ExxonMobil & Friends.

Elsewhere, the amazingly little reported phenomenon known as the Great Pacific Garbage Dump continues to grow. The North Pacific Gyre, an area of ocean currents covering 12.5 *million* square miles, is becoming littered with man-made trash, 90% of which are plastics. Plastics are made of polymers, which are not biodegraded in any practical time scale (think thousands of years). The last 65 years alone have seen this gyre (the worst-littered part is twice an area of Texas) become a dumping ground for discarded items from beer six-pack rings to sandwich wraps to balloons-what will the next 65 years bring? And it is not alone; six other gyres have major debris amounts as well.

The smallest of plastic bits, called nurdles, are manufactured annually in an amount of 5.5 *quadrillion*. Nurdles are being eaten by the smallest oceanic creatures, which in turn are eaten by larger wildlife-and are working their way up the food chain to humans. Many animals (especially birds) are known to die from the plastic infestation; things don't look promising for nearly any species.

But if Republican Sgt Schultzes live blissfully ignorant of the coming travails, its rival party leaders can take solace in the fact that the creatures most resembling Democrats in spinelessness are quite likely quickly taking over the oceans.

> ...things don't look promising for nearly any species.

Jellyfish, who 500 million years ago may have dominated the seas, are again on the march. From the Baltic, Black, and Caspian Seas to the Yellow Sea and Sea of Japan; From the Gulf of Mexico to the coasts of South Africa and Australia, invasive species have replaced other types of fish, multiplying at often stupendous rates.

"We've overfished virtually every resource in the oceans" writes Australian Climate Commission Chief Tim Flannery in the *New York Review of Books* (September 26, 2013), "causing the outright collapse of many ecosystems."

Additionally, by our inadvertent sending of discarded plastic to the oceans, we've created what Flannery calls "splendid little nurseries" for jellyfish growth. Jellyfish polyps (what eggs first turn into) love to latch onto hard surfaces, and the more man-placed items (from piers to oil platforms to simple discarded products) there are, the better it is for the jellies.

Finally, the acidification of the oceans (a 30% increase in the last 30 years) is hurting all shellfish. But jellyfish, with their Democrat-like non-backbones, are unaffected by the change.

Why is jellyfish proliferation so problematic? Besides helping deplete seafood humans depend upon, a number of jellyfish species have poisonous stings that can kill a person in as little as two minutes. Death-by-jellyfish is already hurting beach tourism in many areas. Large groups have clogged power plants and enormous ships; in one instance 40 million Filipinos were left without power thanks to a few tons of jellies trapped in a power plant cooling system.

All truth, said Schopenhauer, goes through three stages. First it is ridiculed. Then it is violently opposed. Then it is accepted as self-evident. Man's insatiable need to consume ever more of nature's bounty now upsets the delicate balance that has evolved over millions of years. Unless MICMAC and its lesser counterparts in the other major countries accelerate rapidly from stage two to stage three of Schopenhauer's system, future evolution on earth may take place without the philosopher's own species in tow.

-September 2013

Chapter Twenty-seven

Unholy Trinity

Occupy Wall Street chose the most recent Sept. 17 to begin its protest against the ills of our current society. It prefaces its Declaration document with stark words: "We come to you at a time when corporations, which place profit over people, self-interest over justice, and oppression over equality, run our governments." A Tea Party then, for those able to sift through the dense corporatized media fog. It is growing and will continue to do so because it intuitively understands at least two of Condor's Unholy Trinity of ideological beliefs underpinning the elites who run the U.S.

First, *that markets are rational and assign prices rationally.* In 1970, the CEOs of the largest 100 U.S. corporations made 45 times what the average worker did. By 2008 that figure was 1081 (this is not a misprint). Capitalism on steroids came at precisely the same moment in history when the financialization of our economy shifted into high gear. In 1970 the largest bank accounted for less than 3 percent of our GDP. Today, the largest six banks comprise 63 percent of GDP. Too big to fail, these banks are too big to exist. That they need to be broken up by Barack Obama ala Teddy Roosevelt and the trusts is not difficult to comprehend. That doing so will not be easy is punctuated by the fact that Wall Street figures now litter the top echelons of government.

The second belief is that *the U.S. must police the world for the safety of its citizens.* This is the greatest ruse since P. T. Barnum. Sacrificing our reputation throughout the globe, our economic prosperity, and the document Franklin signed have become nonissues for our ever expanding military, which is larger than the next 17 combined. We now have unmanned aerial vehicles, or drones, that kill suspected militants in Pakistan and other countries, frequently hitting civilians (aka "collateral damage"). We just assassinated by drone an American citizen in Yemen, denying him a trial and rendering the Fifth Amendment worthless. The U.S. Air Force now trains more drone operators than actual pilots; research and development on manned aircraft has been virtually stopped. But for those worried about neglect of our cities, police departments will within a few years be using drones to issue speeding tickets from directly above our vehicles. No word yet on what kind of witnesses they will make when citations are challenged in court.

The third belief of the elites (one that is perhaps only partially grasped by OWS) is that *environmental and ecological destruction of the planet is manageable.* A century ago, with one billion people, exploitation of Earth's untapped resources was not foreseeably problematic. But in the past 50 years the world economy has grown fivefold, and this month planetary population hits seven billion. Two billion of these live on less that $2 per day.

But we other five billion leave an ecological footprint of 30 percent to 50 percent more each year than what the earth can replenish, and rapid growth in India and China suggests the rate will only increase. So our way of life under the capitalist growth model will soon hit Tim Jackson's wall that reads: "An ever expanding economy divided into a finite planet does not compute."

In the meantime, President Obama Hamlets over whether to allow the Alberta tar sands to be pipelined to the Gulf of Mexico. If he does, the world's leading climatologist James Hansen says, it's "game over" for the planet's climate as we know it. No stakes have ever been higher. Predictably, no story has been more ignored by mainstream media.

Can our "democratic" two-party system save us? Unlikely. Between 1955 and 1961 the Senate filibuster was used one time to block the legislation the majority wanted. In 2009 and 2010, this device was used 84 times. The elites know they only need to own a small part of the government to control all of it. Though an overwhelming majority of Americans favored increased taxation of millionaires to pay down our debt, no tax will pass. Most favor a withdrawal from the Afghanistan quagmire, but nothing will change there either. This is broken government at its most fundamental meaning.

The fear of the elites, though, for the vast waste they've laid to our nation and world, is palpable. A perfect example is the $4.6 million "gift" bestowed on the New York City Police Foundation earlier this year by J. P. Morgan Chase, the world's largest public company. The message is clear: Protect us from the rabble, and we'll cut you in for a nice slice of the pie now shrinking for everyone but us. The cauldron thus begins to boil.

-October 2011

Another MICMAC Attack

"The U.S. government exists primarily for the protection of multinational corporations."

-Robert Scheer

"Crime Doesn't Pay" is an FBI slogan which dates back to the late 1920s, in an era when Al Capone's Chicago bootlegging empire amassed him revenues reportedly worth $60 million in 1927 alone. The Feds went after Capone in two ways: 1) for violating Prohibition's Volstead Act (agent Eliot Ness and his "Untouchables") and 2) for tax evasion. Convicted of crimes via the second avenue, Capone eventually was sentenced to 11 years in prison.

It is slightly preposterous to imagine a newspaper headline from the late 1920s that reads "Capone Offers $3 Million to End Bootlegging Probe." Yet on September 25, 2013, the *Wall Street Journal*'s lead story was "J.P Morgan Offers $3 *Billion* to End Mortgage Probes" (emphasis mine). The story listed the numerous criminal and civil allegations the U.S. government was pursuing against Morgan Chase, and that Morgan CEO Jamie "Cufflinks" Dimon was negotiating his way out of further troubles. One week previous, Morgan paid $920 million to U.S. and U.K. regulators because it had misled them (i.e. lied) regarding its $6 billion "Whale Trader" loss of 2012.

Two days later, the *Journal* reported that, in an unprecedented move, U.S. Attorney General Eric Holder met with Dimon to hammer out a settlement, upping Morgan's possible penalty to $11 billion. The sticking point was whether Morgan Chase would admit wrongdoing in its massive fraud schemes. This is nicely done work by Dimon in our contemporary justice system - tossing out his shareholders' money to avoid jail for him and top echelon brethren.

"It is growing and will continue to grow," wrote Condor of the Occupy movement in October 2011. I was right - up to a point. The Occupy protests spread to hundreds of cities throughout the U.S. and around the globe in the last months of that year. Though at first MICMAC media refused to cover the events, it then did so by emphasizing untruths such as the movement's aims were "vague." Actually, Occupy spokesperson were quite specific in their demands that 1) banking regulations be tightened, 2) high frequency trading be banned, and 3) banksters responsible for the 2008 crash be prosecuted.

Naïve? Absolutely. Congress was not about to reign in its masters. The fact that roughly two-thirds of the protesters were fully employed (and another 18% employed part-time) made certain long-term encampments in parks via tents was not realistic. However, unknown at the time was the extent to which Big Brother was not only watching, but actually disrupting, the Occupy movement.

Documents later obtained (in December 2012) by the Partnership For Civil Justice Fund under the Freedom of Information Act reveal how coordinated the attacks on Occupy were by the FBI, Department of Homeland Security, and local police departments across America. At least six universities were used to access private information of students involved in the movement. But the real story is that the entire surveillance network was done *at the behest and on behalf of the largest multinational corporations* with familiar U.S. names.

A virtually unknown entity called the Domestic Alliance Security Council, a government/corporate alliance created in 2005 (at the request of gigantic companies) to "bridge the information divide between America's public and private sectors," went into high gear. Despite the Occupy movement's stated nonviolent intentions, and public acknowledgment from law enforcement that it was a peaceful coalition, the DASC treated the protesters as criminal and terrorist threats. Surveillance began over a month before the initial protest.

The Council has 200 corporate members; 29 sit on its leadership board including 3M, American Express, Barclays, Archer Daniels Midland, Bank of America, Boeing, Citigroup, Merck, Walmart, Walt Disney, Time Warner, and General Electric. The last three mentioned own (or did at the time in GE's case) ABC, CNN, and NBC - MICMAC media at its finest. No mention of what the DSAC was up to was ever reported; as Naomi Wolfe wrote in the *Guardian* (Dec 30, 2012), "The documents show the cops and DHS working for and with banks to target, arrest, and politically disable American citizens." The Partnership for Civil Justice Funds executive director put it another way, "These documents show these federal agencies functioning as a de facto intelligence arm of Wall Street and Corporate America."

The FBI repeatedly denied the existence of such documents for nearly a year, then remained silent when the files were released.

Oakland was site of one of the longest and most vigorous Occupy protests. There, an under resourced police force in a city on the verge of bankruptcy responded violently to peaceful Occupiers in late 2011. Twelve individuals eventually collected $1 million in compensation for police abuse. No mention of this settlement ever appeared on the airwaves of MICMAC media. The mouthpieces of the Establishment understand that today the FBI's ancient slogan is obsolete, that indeed Crime *Does* Pay, and so does the cover-up of activities performed by one's allies in the Complex. MICMAC members are the new Untouchables.

-September 2013

Chapter Twenty-eight

Wagging the Dog Once More

"God did not create this country to be a nation of followers."

- Mitt Romney
at the Citadel, October 7

"The actions I take will be actions recommended and supported by Israeli leaders."

- Mitt Romney
in Las Vegas, October 18

Last week's Republican National Security Debate, sponsored by Let's Have Another War, Inc. (aka CNN/the Heritage Foundation/ the American Enterprise Institute), focused little or no attention on China, Russia, the Arab Spring, or the Euro crisis. It did, however, predictably pit U.S. Representative Ron Paul vs. the Seven "Attack Iran" Dwarfs.

Among questioners in the select audience, pulled at rogues gallery randomness, were Ahmad Chalabi promoter Danielle Pletka, Fred "Iraq has WMDs" Kagan, Paul "Oil Will Pay for the Iraq War" Wolfowitz, and David "Wiretap without a Warrant" Addington. A more representative quartet of discredited neocons could not be found, Donald Rumsfeld apparently ancient artifact shopping outside Baghdad. As an added bonus Reagan-era fossil Ed "Miranda" Meese was unearthed, reminding many of his immortal maxim, "If a person is innocent of a crime, then he is not a suspect."

Tweaking Meese logic to foreign affairs, it is clear that, in the case of Iran at least, a nation *suspected* of working to acquire nuclear weapons *must* be guilty of said accusation. Never mind that, despite the usual *New York Times* and *Washington Post* hysterics to the contrary, the recent International Atomic Energy Agency report contains, according to experts who've actually read it, no new substantive material. The 2007 U.S. National Intelligence Estimate that stated Iran is not working on a bomb is still intact.

So why the sudden interest in ratcheting up rhetoric against modern Persia? For clues, one must travel both backward and forward in time. In October, a previous entry of the now endless GOP debate scheme took place in the true heart of American-style capitalism – Las Vegas. Romney made his October 18 remarks quoted above regarding possibly changing Israel's capitol to the foreign policy editor of *Yisrael Hayom* (*Israel Today*), owned by big time GOP donor Sheldon Alderson, currently Forbes' eighth richest American and owner of the Venetian and Sands casinos, (which coincidentally hosted the Vegas debate).

Alderson's Israeli paper, started in 2007 as a free daily (like the Moonie *Washington Times*) to help elect Benjamin Netanyahu Prime Minister, is now that country's largest. In Israel foreigners may contribute in party elections – and 75% of Bibi's 2007 campaign loot came from Alderson and other U.S. donors. Mitt and the other four "not invited – Ron Paul" frontrunners thus ran to answer the queries of Yisrael Hayom's interviewer.

Fast forward to next January, when Bibi faces two large hurdles. First, his foreign minister Avigdor "Luca" Lieberman is likely to be indicted for a myriad of reasons including money laundering. Second, Bibi faces a scathing indictment from the state comptroller for the bungled handling of last December's forest fires which killed 44 Israelis. Non-Alderson owned Israeli news editorials now mention the possibility that either of these events may cripple his coalition. This would be a bit embarrassing for the yo-yo U.S. Congress, which in May gave Bibi 29 standing O's in an address before that currently immensely popular (approval rating – 9%) body. Why not, ala Barry Levinson's 90s cult film Wag the Dog, talk of bombing Iran to change headlines?

Rhetoric aside, who could blame Iran if it tried to acquire a nuke? In the last decade it saw "Axis of Evil" partner Iraq (with no nukes) get invaded, while the other member of this trio of David

Frum's imagination, North Korea (with nukes) has received diplomatic treatment instead.

Former CIA analyst Ray McGovern wasn't invited to the Neocon Redux Lovefest last week, but three of his recently posted online questions should be asked of all candidates, including the usually evasive Barack Obama: 1) Do you think we had the right to overthrow the democratically elected leader of Iran in 1953? 2) Assuming Iran gets a nuclear weapon, do you agree with former Defense Secretary Bob Gates who said, "I really think they (the Iranians) would see it in the first instance as a deterrent," or do you think they would commit suicide by firing it at Israel?" 3) How many nukes *does* Israel have?

The last question, due to Israel's official policy of nuclear ambiguity, is generally verboten in the Land of the Free. Ron Paul, unprompted, claimed 200 or 300 during the debate, and none of the Dwarfs challenged him. The reaction from our Corporate Media: total silence. In Truman Show America, 'tis always better to keep the people uninformed of their interests, lest they begin connecting devious dots.

-December 2011

Wait 'Til Next Year!

For only the second time since the 1994 strike, there is no postseason baseball in New York. Major October entertainment in the Big Apple must therefore take the form of Bibi's Traveling Circus - aka Israeli Prime Minister Benjamin Netenyahu's annual United Nations address. On the heels of new Iranian President Hassan Rouhani's overture to thaw relations with the West- something that would appear to be in the interests of Middle East peace and stability - Bibi excoriated Rouhani as a "wolf in sheep's clothing" who was only using his olive branch as a ploy to obtain nuclear weapons.

Bibi and the Boys (Netenyahu's Israeli government circus pals) have by now perfected this routine - and for good reason. They've been using it for decades. This delights MICMAC media, which gets to repeat Israeli allegations verbatim 1) without ever analyzing whether they contain a grain of truth, and 2) knowing that an America more concerned with its fantasy football leagues can't possibly remember ancient predictions about Iran emanating from Israel and its allies. A helpful (and mere sampling) reverse timeline:

In 2009, then candidate for Prime Minister Netenyahu told a U.S. Congressional delegation, "our experts say Iran is probably one or two years away" from acquiring nuclear weapons.

In 2008, Mossad (Israel's CIA) former chief Meir Amit stated Israel has "12 months in which to destroy Iran's nuclear program or risk coming under nuclear attack itself."

On July 11, 2007, Israeli Military Intelligence announced Iran would "cross the nuclear threshold within six months to a year and attain nuclear capability as early as mid-2009."

In 2005, Israel Defense Minister Shoul Mofaz said Iran was "at a point of no return" regarding its nuclear weapons' capability.

On November 17, 2003, then Mossad chief Meir Dagan stated Iran's nukes program was "at a point of no return" within one year and would have "the potential to produce 10 bombs a year."

On July 10, 1996, newly elected Prime Minister Netenyahu addressed the U.S. Congress and said "the deadline for attaining" Iran's goal of acquiring nukes "is getting extremely close."

On November 1, 1995, Netenyahu told the Knesset that "within three to five years, we can assume Iran will become autonomous in its ability to develop and produce a nuclear bomb."

In 1992, U.S. House Republicans released a report stating it was "a 98% certainty Iran had all the components required for two or three nuclear weapons."

In April 1987 *The Washington Post* published an article "Atomic Ayatollahs: Just What the Mideast Needs - an Iranian Bomb," claiming the threat was "imminent."

On June 21, 1951, then twenty month old Bibi Netenyahu announced from his playpen, "Mama, Iran will have nukes by '55" (ok, this one's admittedly apocryphal).

This "Wait 'Til Next Year" rallying cry, possibly borrowed from Brooklyn Dodger fans (whose heroes remained without a World Championship until…1955), has long since grown old. Netenyahu fears an attack from Iranian nukes about as much as Justin

Verlander fears facing a line-up of Bad News Bears. What is really going on here?

First, Israel wishes to maintain dominance in the region, free to do militarily whatever it wants.

Second, it wants international attention diverted from its continued (now 46 years and counting) illegal occupation of the Palestinian West Bank.

Third, its MICMAC allies like to completely obfuscate reality by remaining virtually silent on Israel's own impressive and long standing nuclear weapons program.

Take, for example, that trio of leading U.S. newspapers *The Washington Post, Wall Street Journal,* and *The New York Times,* who might be more accurately termed The Three Stooges of serious slapstick journalism.

The Three Stooges of serious slapstick journalism.

In rehashing Netenyahu's UN speech, the Larry *Post* placed deep within its article the single sentence, "Israel possesses an undeclared nuclear weapons arsenal." Nothing more was added.

The Moe *Journal* was cleverly cryptic. In paragraph eight of its "Netenyahu Assails Iran's New Leader" story, this nugget was nonchalantly inserted: "Iran, which denies its nuclear program is aimed at weapons development, also demanded Israel place its presumed nuclear arsenal under international safeguards and sign the Nuclear Non-Proliferation Treaty." And then instant segue to Iranian "threats."

But the Curly *Times* was most brazen of all. No mention whatsoever was made of Israel's nuclear weapons.

Robert Parry, in response, writes, "If a country with a large but undeclared nuclear arsenal threatens war against a country without a single nuclear bomb, you might think that a serious news organization would note the existing nuclear arsenal at least in passing."

You might also think that the nuclear-armed country's threats be pointed out as violations of the UN Charter (Article II, Paragraph 4). Or that when *The Guardian* in September revealed that the NSA routinely shares raw data of US citizens with Israel, our national "Newspaper of Record" might follow-up or at least reprint these explosive facts.

But in the cases of Israel's threats and nukes, and the US government trampling on its own citizens' rights – for the *New York Times* and cohorts – it's "Nyuk, nyuk, nyuk."

-October 2013

Chapter Twenty-nine

The Magnificent Seven

*If destruction be our lot,
we must ourselves
Be its author and finisher.
As a nation of freeman,
We must live through all
time, or die by suicide.*

–**Abraham Lincoln,**
1838

Suicide is painless.

–*Theme from M*A*S*H*,*
1970

Seventy years to the week after Japan's sneak attack on Pearl Harbor, indefatigable and high minded Michigan Senator Carl Levin, along with sidekick John McCain of Arizona, may have conducted a similar maneuver on the U.S. Constitution both have sworn to support and defend. Amendments to Senate Bill 1867, aka the National Defense Authorization Act for 2012, were reportedly crafted in secret by the two Armed Services Committee ranking members just prior to the weekend most Americans stuff themselves with stuffing, riot to obtain better deals on flat screen TVs, and then actively participate in battle (via fantasy leagues and those flat screens), with their beloved gridiron gladiators, through overtime if needed. No committee hearing was held, no notice to other committee heads (such as jurisdictional Judiciary or Intelligence) was given.

Senate Bill 1867 now includes sections (S 1031 and S 1032)* which authorizes the military, upon order of the President, to arrest and indefinitely detain American citizens, even on U.S. soil, without trial or even charge. Here is the language of 1031 (b) (2) "A person who was a part of or *substantially supported* al-Qaeda, the Taliban, or *associated forces* that are engaged in hostilities against the United States or its coalition partners... (emphasis added), and (c) (1) "Detention under the law of war without trial until the end of hostilities authorized by the Authorization for Use of Military Force (AUMF)."

Section 1032 *allows* (but does not mandate) that even U.S. citizens on U. S. soil accused of Terrorism be held by the military rather than be charged by the civilian court system.

Key phrases "substantially supported" and "associated forces" are expansions of the original AUMF declaration and could conceivably mean any number of unsuspecting people. "Until the end of hostilities," of course, means never, since the scenario of someone named Tommy T. Terrorist signing surrender documents to any Douglas MacArthur successor is highly doubtful at best.

Though the language of 1031 and 1032 is not crystal clear, any ambiguity was alleviated by Levin/McCain water boy Lindsey "Low Han-ded" Graham, who proclaimed on the Senate floor, "Section 1031, the statement of authority to detain, does apply to American citizens and it designates the world as the battlefield, including the homeland."

Utah's Mark Udall offered an amendment to SB 1867 to take out S 1031, but it failed by a 38-60 vote, just enough votes needed to avoid a filibuster by some Jefferson Smith-type who might attempt to awaken a slumbering populace. Then California's Dianne Feinstein proposed another to exempt U.S. citizens from the 2001 AUMF; that failed 45-55.

In the end, The World's Greatest Deliberative Body voted 93-7 to codify the negation of Article III, Section 3 (1) of the Constitution ("No Person shall be convicted of Treason unless on the Testimony of Two Witnesses to the same overt Act, or on Confession in open Court."), as well as the 5th Amendment Due Process clause. Voting for the previously cherished American values were Republicans Tom Coburn (OK) Mike Lee(UT) and Rand Paul(KY), Democrats Tom Harkin(IA), Jeff Merkley (OR) and Ron Wyden(OR), and Independent Bernie Sanders(VT).

Like the hired guns who saved the tiny village from Mexican marauders in the immortal western *The Magnificent Seven*, this heroic heptagon tried to rescue the village of America from the bandits whose regular extortion of the citizenry has gone on quite long enough. Unfortunately, real life is not like the movies, unless *Triumph of the Will* is to be soon reenacted in Atlanta (Sister City to Nuremberg). Though Team Obama has threatened to veto the bill, the Senate may of course override with a 2/3rds vote. If it does, so goes another nail in the coffin of our soon-to-be former Republic.

Are Sections 1031 and 1032 even about fear of al-Qaeda? Why, after a decade of its War on a Tactic, and when al-Qaeda has been officially declared "operationally ineffective" in Af-Pak, does growth in executive power continue? The answer may lie in cities across America where the Occupied Movement has pitched its tents. The fear in Washington of rebellion is real, and so is the fear that a growing number of voters are on to its gilded game of graft. *This Week* (ABC) and *Meet the Press* (NBC), those Sunday morning "issues" infomercials brought to you by corporate do-gooders like Boeing, Chase, and Exxon Mobil, both neglected to mention Senate Bill 1867 in the week after debate and passage. Not an oversight, folks, - they just don't want us getting all worked up over losing our basic rights. Now back to the Lions' playoff chances, on our 80" screens...

-December 2011

---

* Note: Sections 1031 and 1032 eventually were written into law as sections 1021 and 1022.

The 33% Majority

Within the bubble that consists of Truman Show America, there are varying degrees of illusion. Some dogged climbers appear to get close to the exit walls, only to retreat comfortably back into the Show's confines. Most people walk atop the earth's surface, struggling, as they go about their daily lives, to process the overwhelming and numbing amounts of data spewed forth nonstop by mighty MICMAC. Since the financial meltdown of 2008, though, a strange new mutant group of humans has emerged politically as they have simultaneously submerged into the depths of the earth, removing themselves from any connection to reality.

These are the Teabaggers of the so-called Tea Party movement. Ostensibly formed as an anti-spending, anti-federal deficit group, the Teabaggers curiously had no problem with George W Bush's tripling of the debt or profligate spending on ruinous wars while cutting taxes for the rich. Once Barack Obama entered office though, these mostly white, mostly older, and mostly well-off persons became energized and, through a constant publicity machine created at Fox "News," began to enter the public consciousness, and also the Republican Party.

Largely (secretly) funded by the leaders of climate change denial, the billionaire top ten U.S. air polluting Koch brothers, the Teabaggers most resemble (intellectually at least) the Morlocks of H.G. Wells' 1895 science fiction novel *The Time Machine*. These distant future troglodyte underground dwellers were extremely sensitive to light; the Teabaggers, oddly more bewildered than other Americans by decades of MICMAC pronouncements, are little capable of seeing the light of reason, even as it shines brilliantly upon their globally warmed craniums during infrequent sojourns to the planet's surface.

Having infiltrated a decaying Republican Party left in shambles by the Bush/Cheney/Rumsfeld junta, The Tea Party took a major step forward, if not quite operational control, after the 2012 elections. The Affordable Care Act, aka Obamacare, a seriously flawed but duly passed healthcare reform law judged constitutional by a corporate-friendly Supreme Court, proved the trigger for building a Teabagger firewall against any modicum of government functionality.

On October 1, 2013, the U.S. government did, in fact, shutdown, at least partially, with the Republican-controlled House of Representatives unwilling to any longer fund it without steep cuts to social benefits for millions of their fellow citizens (but without considering a penny of raised taxes for billionaires). More proof thus provided, if any was needed, that this body in no way actually represents the populace it is by constitutional law designed to. It was a partial shutdown, for 16 days, because some services continued, while others did not.

Services deemed essential included 1) uninterrupted congressional pay 2) keeping open the congressional gymnasium, complete with heated pool and flat-screen TVs 3) NSA surveillance on Americans (though FOIA requests by watchdog groups into potential NSA illegal activities were deemed non-essential and halted) and 4) military operations in Libya and Somalia. The Pentagon, in fact, anticipating the October 1 shutdown, went on a $63 billion contract spending spree in September - over twice what it had averaged the previous two months.

Services thought nonessential, and thus eliminated during the shutdown, included 1) nutritional aid for low income children 2) funding for domestic violence protection, 3) help for cancer-stricken kids hoping for experimental treatment from the National Institute of Health 4) Ninety-four percent of EPA inspections, thus giving some breathing space for delighted major toxic waste providers (i.e. Koch Industries).

On October 16, one day from putting the United States of America, owner of the world's reserve currency, in default, an event which economists across the ideological spectrum and around the globe deemed would result

"It's hard not to believe the lunatics have taken over the asylum."

in financial Armageddon, the House finally voted 285-144 to raise the nation's debt ceiling and avoid default. As Congress threatened this action, *The Australian*, a rightwing Rupert Murdoch-founded sister paper to *The Wall Street Journal*, editorialized that "It's hard not to believe the lunatics have taken over the asylum."

One hundred forty-four members of the House (all Republicans), precisely 33% of the current 432 member body, voted to put the U.S. in default. They are 62% of the Republican caucus, or roughly the same percentage that holds on to climate change denial as a basic tenet of faith. Most disbelieve in evolution as well.

How did this happen? Through an obscene gerrymandering of districts that allowed the GOP to retake the House in 2012 despite 1.4 million more votes cast nationwide for Democrats. Add to that the informal so-called Hastert rule, by which Speaker John Boehner refused to allow legislation to come to the House floor without the support of a majority of his Republican caucus. A perfect recipe was thus provided for government by minority.

The Morlock champion to crawl up from the earth's mantle in this fiasco is Princeton and Harvard educated Senator Ted Cruz of Texas, who filibustered Obamacare for 21 hours in September. The civil war now unleashed in the GOP has made right-wing Speaker Boehner all but fatally wounded by the new and even more extreme element of his party. In *The Time Machine*, the Morlocks did battle with the passive, clueless, and cowardly surface-dwelling Eloi, a futuristic embodiment of what's left of the non-Teabagging GOP.

The current Morlock-Eloi fight is a portent of the coming political disintegration. Another debt ceiling deadline arrives in less than four months, and Cruz is riding high with bountiful campaign gifts and being allowed to pollute MICMAC airwaves on the Sunday talk shows. As the *Borowitz Report* accurately opines, "Senator Cruz's dream of keeping poor people from seeing a doctor must never die."

-October 2013

Chapter Thirty

How to Know a Good Terrorist

The Truman Show, America's longest running program of fear, this week quietly celebrated its 65th birthday. Condor's mnemonically unimpaired readers will recall that on Feb. 27, 1947, Michigan GOP Senator Arthur Vandenberg told Democratic President Harry Truman that the only way to get a massive military buildup a mere eighteen months after World War II's end was to "scare hell" out of the country. "Give 'em Hell"

"Give 'em Hell" Harry Promptly obliged...

Harry promptly obliged; his Truman Doctrine speech pledged to fight communism anywhere and everywhere on earth.

The Show's ratings took a temporary hit in 1991 (with the Soviet Union collapse), creating some panic among MICMAC officials, but al-Qaeda's appearance later in the decade assured long term commitments from all concerned Show sponsors.

A curious twist occurred in Episode 780 (that's one for each month since early 1947). On Feb. 9, NBC reported a story that Israel's secret service Mossad has collaborated with Mujahideen e-Khalq (MEK), an Iranian dissident group, to assassinate five Iranian scientists since 2007. These attacks allegedly were done to help dissuade Iran from building nuclear weapons, long a defining goal of Israeli foreign policy. Two high ranking U.S. officials anonymously confirmed the story.

Assassinating Iranian scientists in this fashion poses a small technical problem for the Israelis and their public cheerleaders in the U.S. (Congress and mainstream media). According to the U.S. State Department, MEK is an officially designated Foreign Terrorist

Organization. Founded in the 1960s on Marxist and anti-Western principles, MEK has been long associated with violent incidents and cult-like behavior. It has reportedly killed U.S. military advisors and attacked U.S. diplomats.

Strangely, MEK's terrorist tag has not prevented some high profile U.S. politicians from speaking on its behalf. *The Christian Science Monitor* reported last August that former governors Ed Rendell (PA) and Howard Dean (VT), retired General Wesley Clark, ex-NYC mayor Rudy Guiliani, and Bush II CIA Director Michael Hayden were among those receiving from $10,000 to $50,000 per speech to preach the Gospel of MEK Reformation. Clark and Guiliani were predictably seen last Friday on CNN's *Erin Burnett Outfront* trumpeting the Iranian nuclear threat. Unfortunately for their credibility, the *New York Times* reported the next day that the consensus of all 16 U.S. intelligence agencies still says there is no hard evidence Iran is working on building nukes.

The State Department is in a difficult position. It can 1) cave in to the highly paid shills and take MEK off the Terror list, which will infuriate legitimate Iranian dissident groups like the Green Movement (the well publicized 2009 Tehran protesters); 2) prosecute the likes of Dean and Guiliani for providing material support to terrorists (about as likely as the Cubs winning the 2012 World Series); or 3) teach Americans how to distinguish between good and bad terrorists. We are well trained to know that other designated FTOs Hezbollah and Hamas are bad, so we need indoctrination as to why a cult-like band of loonies with deep pockets who routinely killed Americans in the not-so-distant past are now good.

The Truman Show is presently showing noticeable signs of the rapidly aging process. Soon senility may set in among the scriptwriters. Dean, in response to NBC's story, astonishingly stated, "Either the source committed treason, or committed the usual Washington sin of lying to the press." In other words, if the report is accurate (and only MEK has denied it) we have a former Presidential candidate opining it is treason for U.S. officials to leak the truth about one foreign nation's assassinations of another's scientists, assassinations which are escalating the possibility of U.S. involvement into yet another Middle East war. Since we may presume Dean is currently incapable of coherent foreign policy thought, it is obvious his scriptwriters have glaring holes in their narrative. Perhaps, before $5 per gallon gas becomes normalized here, a fourth option, that of pulling the plug on this long-running farcical serial, may be in order. Who knows, replacing it with a program based on the quaint old Constitution might attract some loyal viewers, too.

-February 2012

Good Terrorist Update

On September 28, 2012, the U.S. State Department removed the Mujahedeen e-Khalq (MEK) organization from its list of terrorist groups. The State Department said that in doing so it "does not overlook or forget the MEK's past acts of terrorism, including its involvement in the killing of U.S. citizens in Iran in the 1970s and an attack on U.S. soil in 1992." But State said that the MEK had now renounced acts of violence.

> **But State said that the MEK had now renounced acts of violence.**

As Ned Beatty's character said in the 1986 comedy *Back to School*, which saw Rodney Dangerfield as Thornton Mellon allowed to attend Beatty's university with zero academic credentials in exchange for funding a new business school, "In all fairness, it was a *really big check* Mr. Mellon wrote."

So, in all fairness to the U.S. officials, Democrat and Republican alike, who were paid to mouthpiece for the new former terrorists, they *were really big checks* given to them by said terrorists. One might even say we currently live in a Check Republic.

−November 2013

Europe on the Brink

The story of the world's economy over the past decade begins with the fact that, in 2002, total global debt was $84 trillion. Today, even after the financial crisis of 2008-09, it has risen to $195 trillion. Seeing that worldwide GDP is $65 trillion, we have an exact 3 to 1 debt-to-GDP ratio-higher today than at the height of that crisis.

The debt has been run up by people, corporations, and especially governments-sovereign nations (though perhaps not sovereign for long). Greece, as everyone by now knows, has gotten so far in the red its angry citizens may soon petition a move to Mars. Its railway system alone costs seven times to operate what its annual revenues generate. Severe cuts affecting the living standards of that tiny member of the Eurozone have been imposed by Euro financial authorities. In truth, as *Airplane's* Ted Striker would say, "It's worse than Detroit."

But the much larger economies of Spain and Italy are now teetering toward Greek-style chaos. Spain's unemployment has hit nearly 24%; the *Wall Street Journal* reported April 19 that the two nations' banks had little of the cash left from a generous lending program given by the European Central Bank's (ECB) Long-Term Refinancing Operation.

The program worked like this: unlimited amounts of liquidity were provided for member banks for up to three years, at a rate of 1% (that's right- ONE percent). Italian and Spanish banks then invested the amounts borrowed in their own country's bonds, frequently getting above 4%. This enabled them to generate handsome short-term profits (dubbed "the Sarkozy carry trade," in honor of the French President likely to lose reelection May 6 to a Socialist, further unnerving markets).

But that money is now nearly gone. Experts say the banks will have to stop buying the sovereign bonds, or sell bonds to raise needed cash. Either way, the international community will have to step in, and on April 20 the International Monetary Fund (the world's lender of last resort) announced, without U.S. help, a near doubling of its war chest for "the impending crisis."

Of course, had the plan pushed by financial guru George Soros been adopted, the present threat may have been averted. Soros (and various others) proposed insuring the ECB against solvency risk on newly issued Italian and Spanish treasury bills bought from commercial banks. Banks could have then held on to the T-bills as cash equivalents, allowing Spain and Italy to refinance their debt at close to 1%. This would have protected both countries from the coming likely Greek default, as well as their own internal hemorrhaging. But the banking-bought ruling elite opted otherwise.

The most frightening aspect of all this, practically unacknowledged until now, is what will happen to what's left of European sovereignty once the European Stability Mechanism takes effect (expected in July). The articles of the ESM read like a complete surrender of individual nations' financial independence. Article 9 states, "ESM members hereby irrevocably and unconditionally undertake to pay on demand any capital call made on them within seven days." Article 27 says ESM property, funding, and assets are "immune from search (and) seizure…by executive, judicial, administrative, or judicial action." Article 30 enables *anyone* associated with the ESM to be "immune from the legal process with respect to acts performed by them." The fund will start with 500 billion euros ($655 billion), but more will undoubtedly be needed. And the banks will stay in control.

The ECB president responsible for the latest bailout? Why, former Goldman Sachs Europe VP Mario Draghi. Like Hank Paulsen, the ex-Goldman CEO who as U.S. Treasury Secretary rescued his industry pals in 2008, Mario remembers well from whence he came. We would do well to remember that the monumentally incorrect mathematical models which told us that tons of no income/no job mortgagors being unable to make their house payments at the same time was a "25 sigma event"-meaning as unlikely as winning a national lottery twenty-one times in a row-was brought to us by none other than the good folks at Goldman Sachs. More asinine calculations have seldom been made. Less fallout for such stupidity has never been equaled.

—April 2012

America beyond the Brink

The 2013 Forbes list of the world's billionaires tallies 442 Americans (out of 1426), compared to 129 (out of 376) in 1995. That was the year after the North American Free Trade Agreement took effect-the pact between Canada, Mexico, and the United States to help create jobs for all three nations. Instead, NAFTA became the catalyst for a hemispheric race to the bottom regarding jobs, wages, and environmental protection. It did, however, help gift us the World's Richest Person, Mexican telecom emperor Carlos Slim ($73 billion). In a nation who average per capita income is less that $14,500, Slim must be a fulfilling source of pride.

Though Bill Gates ($67 billion) holds onto the Richest American moniker, the families with the greatest concentrations of wealth now are the four Waltons (of Walmart-combined $107 billion worth) and the deadly duo Koch Brothers (Koch Industries-combined $68 billion). Walmart is the world's largest retailer and second largest public corporation. To amass the Waltons' great fortunes it has helped immensely that wages for their 2.2 million employees be kept below the median of the retail sector. Full-time Walmart employees earn about $26,000 per year. Of course, the company makes sure one-third of its workforce are given under 30 hours per week so that it can avoid doling out health care benefits it prefers not to pay. Walmart has externalized costs so well, in the form of using cheap foreign supplied goods made with near slave labor, and also paying three year veteran customer service managers $14,000 who must receive subsidized (by the taxpayers) housing to survive, that it can afford to pay its

CEO a $20.7 million annual salary. This figure is something the average Walmart employee can aspire to as well, if he or she only works, at present pay, another 785 years.

The Koch brothers, whose business consists of extracting from the ground and selling the maximum amount of nonrenewable fossil fuels possible while allowing everyone else on earth to pay the costs of its theft, pollution, and the destabilizing climate change resulting from its activities, have been politically influential long before becoming universally infamous. Spurred on by the nefarious 1971 "Powell Memo," an advisory to big business letter written by soon-to-be U.S. Supreme Court Justice Lewis Powell to anesthetize higher education's anti-free market bias, right-wing titans like the Kochs, Joseph Coors, Richard Mellon Scaife and others began funding "think tanks" like the American Enterprise Institute, Heritage Foundation, and Koch Foundations to give cover to their wish for the destruction of any public oversight of private enterprise. Their wish has largely come true.

...Koch companies have been found guilty in numerous criminal and civil actions...

Over the past two decades, Koch companies have been found guilty in numerous criminal and civil actions, including stealing 300 million gallons of oil from public and Indian lands through fraudulent measuring (known as "The Koch Method"), and yet cause no rupture in the Brothers' ever expanding wealth.

Elsewhere, at the neutered-by-corporations major universities, presidents now act as little more than chief fundraisers. Condor's own Michigan State University may no longer be "little brother" to its rival the University of Michigan on the football field (having now won five of the last six meetings), but it still is where matters count the most-the university endowment. Though MSU is one of only 69 colleges or universities with an over $1 billion endowment fund (49th at $1.4 billion), it pales to U of M's $7.7 billion (7th in the U.S.).

Therefore, to save money, it must cut corners-like refusing to pay 35 teaching assistants for summer classes taught, saving it $100,000. Unfortunately, the negative publicity generated by the protesting graduate students, who have grieved the university's scrooge-like approach, came just before school officials' lavish overseas trips to watch basketball games, paid by MSU, was exposed by a local television reporter. In other words, let the student workers starve, but priorities must be maintained.

Also emulating what might be referred to as the Billionaires Clubs are the popular franchises of our National Pastime. Bloomberg News reported in October that ten of the 30 major league baseball teams are valued at over $1 billion apiece. These include the San Francisco Giants, World Series winners in both 2010 and 2012. To get to the sport's Valhalla, the Giants have paid their players considerably well-a $142 million team payroll in 2013. Unfortunately for many working in the organization-belts need to be tightened to pay, for instance, pitcher Barry Zito's $126 million contract over seven years that included zero above average seasons; one rating system listed Zito 296th of 305 MLB pitchers for 2013. So the Giants are one of two teams (the Miami Marlins are the other) being grieved by employees rather ungratefully asking to make the minimum wage of $7.25/hour.

With the Labor Department stating that questionable pay practices are "endemic to the industry" including improper use of unpaid interns, the Giants have already paid $545,000 in back wages to 74 non-player personnel. San Fran also recently settled with security guards for $500,000 to compensate for back and overtime pay claims. Fans will happily note that the club will pay Zito $7 million in 2014 to *not pitch*, having quickly declined its final year option on the southpaw known as Planet Zito, rather than the $18 million it was obligated for had it exercised the option.

Two current players, Clayton Kershaw and Robinson Cano, are reportedly in the $300 million range for new contracts.* Cano asked for $305 million from the New York Yankees (team worth-$3.28 billion), and Kershaw reportedly turned down a like sum from the ($2.1 billion) Los Angeles Dodgers. Four decades ago, Condor's favorite Detroit Tiger, (and future Hall of Fame) outfielder Al Kaline, turned down a $100,000 annual salary for a different reason-because he didn't feel he deserved that much. Such humility and class are no longer salient features in today's celebrity/sports culture. But the absurdity of present-day wealth inequality causes barely an eye blink in Truman Show America. Collapsing societies never understand what's truly happening around them until it's too late.

−November 2013

---

*   Cano eventually "settled" for a $240 million ten year contract with the Seattle Mariners. Kershaw, who is staying with the Dodgers, will scrape by with $215 million for seven years.

IN CONCLUSION

In principio erat Verbum (John 1:1)

Chapter Thirty-two

Buttons and Bows

Four score and eleven years ago Hollywood released *The Four Horsemen of the Apocalypse*, 1921's top grossing film and one that made Valentino an overnight star. Four score minus forty years ago, Young Condor memorably (for him if no one else) phoned his favorite befuddled movie show host to assist him recite on-air the names of Notre Dame's famed backfield, inspiringly tagged shortly after the film's release. Bill Kennedy (at the Movies) was featuring *Knute Rockne All American* and was stumped, per usual, by another caller's query. As most Catholic school boys of a certain time and place once knew- Crowley, Layden, Miller, and Stuhldreyer were the gridiron horseback heroes.

Four decades hence, Condor Had a Dream-of a different quartet. This vision's contents are addressed to all present day Bill Kennedys (Note: All italicized language that follows is taken from the Book of Revelation, King James Bible, 1789 edition):

> *And I saw when the Lamb opened one of the seals, and I heard, as it were the noise of thunder, one of the four beasts saying, come and see.*
>
> *And I saw, and behold a white horse: and he that sat on him had a bow; and a crown was given onto him: and he went forth conquering and to conquer.*

And the rider of the white horse was named Madison, and the bow that was given unto him was a Sacred Document, and the crown was Justice, and he went forth conquering by shining example the world of thinking mankind, and this gilded paper worked well for a Course of years; but then it began to falter, and by and by the people lost faith in what was Sacred, and lo one day didst permit the assassination of its fellow citizens, and their indefinite detention, and warrantless searches, and secret evidence routinely accepted by its learned judges, and war crimes including (torture by any other name is still) torture; and a continuous surveillance of itself, and extraordinary rendition to totalitarian regimes, and all this to "protect" the very same citizens; and in plain view of a million and more trained in law, who had each sworn an oath to support this Constitution, but who had become too preoccupied, or fearful, or corrupted, or had fallen asleep at their mahogany desks.

And there went out another horse that was red: and power was given to him that sat thereon to take peace from the earth, and that they should kill one another: and there was given unto him a great sword.

And he that sat upon this horse, red from the rivers of blood it was so soaked in, was named POTUS, and the power that was given unto him was the most dread weapon in human history, and the killing was thence done, twice unleashed to demonstrate its terrible warning and wrath, and in the far corners of the earth were those pursued by the sword and the threat of the Great Sword, with its capacity to destroy the earth many times over, and POTUS continued to carry the Big Stick, this "Football," this "Button," by his side at all times, and he alone would choose when to execute.

And when he had opened the third seal, I heard the third beast say, come and see. And I beheld, and lo a black horse; and he that sat on him had a pair of balances in his hand. And I heard a voice in the midst of the four beasts say, a measure of wheat for a penny, and three measures of barley for a penny; and see thou hurt not the oil and the wine.

And the black horse was ridden by one named Goldman, and Goldman created its own commodities index, and the speculation from the wheat and the rice and the corn and the sugar and the livestock earned it billions upon billions of profits, and because of the index, and the other indexes it inspired, prices rose so that hundreds of millions starved, but POTUS and his vassals allowed it so, and not a word from those who could expose and denounce such evil.

And when he had opened the fourth seal, I heard the voice of the fourth beast say, Come and see. And I looked, and behold a pale (green) horse, and his name that sat on him was Death, and Hell followed with him.

And the green horse was the earth itself, and its sublime but delicate ecology, and the Death which rode the horse beyond its strength, for greed and profit and plunder, and turned it pale after the slumber of the lawyers and the bursting of the bombs and the stealing of the multitude's food and water (which was needed for mere subsistence), and the drainage of an oil of a different kind, continued so until the earth bucked in thunderous fury, and *"every mountain and island were moved out of their places."*

And then I awoke from the dream, and observed and remembered the immense goodness and bravery and ingenuity and kindheartedness of this confused people, and knew instantly that all things were indeed possible, and that my fellow slumberers could also be awakened before it was too late, and that when they did some new and good from among their midst would arise and slay this pestilence of ignorance, and see reality, and would not then, in the words of dying Europe's greatest living gift to America, "experience the absolute despair of an unthinking modernity, but rediscover a world where things have meaning."

—February 2012.

Sacred Violence

Violence is unrelenting. Around the world, both between and within nations, humans lash out in violent revenge-it's always revenge-or preemptive strikes, or now preventative strikes (send in the drones), always justified by one side for fear of what the other may do or to pay back for what the other has done. This cycle has gone on for thousands of years; millions have been killed so that others may live in a limited peace. These homicides have happened since the dawn of man.

Rene Girard, the French-born cultural critic who taught four decades at several elite U.S. universities, has traced the common thread to the beginnings of human culture. Stories throughout the world tell of mythical gods who come down to earth and give men wisdom or things needed for men to survive. These "gods" of early societies, states Girard, represent a truth distorted by later generations who couldn't collectively face what had actually happened at the myths' genesis.

All human desire, according to Girard, is *mimetic*. Mimesis, or imitation, leads to rivalry, which in turn leads to conflict, which often results in violence. Tribal violence grows into *all against all* violence. When *all against all* violence occurs, ancient societies did often not survive. But some, namely those who became our ancestors, did. The mechanism that enabled primitive cultures to save themselves from self-destruction was the *scapegoat*, or *victim par excellence*, a person either an outsider to the tribe or one easily distinguishable from the others within it by some deformity or physical handicap.

All against all violence thus transformed into *all against one* violence. One individual could be killed, or sacrificed, and the contagion of violence be pacified. The people then came to see the one killed as divine, since he had miraculously "stopped" the violence from spreading. And tribes began to reenact this event to thwart future outbreaks of contagious violence. This is how ritual began. Ritual grew from myth. And myth is grounded in reality.

Ritual and sacrifice, Girard convincingly argues in *Violence and the Sacred* (1972) are at the origins of every religion. We are thus, all men and women, the children of religion.

> *People of another (earlier) world were living in a village. They knew a new world was going to be formed. One day a number of them started to quarrel. One of the number was North Star. The others fell on him, meaning to kill him, but he fled and soared into the sky. All started after, but when they saw they could not get him: "Well," they said, "let him be. He is North Star. He will be of use to the people of the world that is to come, as a guide by night to their travels."*
>
> *-Tale of Montagnais Innu people of eastern Quebec, neighbor and rival to the Micmac.*

On the other side of the world, in India, there is a Hindu Veda myth concerning *Purusha*, who Girard writes, is "the archetypical man who is a little larger than the universe and is put to death by a crowd of sacrificers. Since he is the primordial man, we wonder where the crowd could have come from. It is from this murder that all reality emerges" (Girard, *Battling to the End*, p. 135).

At the center of both cited myths is an outcast from society, chased off a cliff in one, and torn to pieces in the other, who becomes divinized over time. These are myths of collective murder. They differ not, at their root, from the Greek myths of Oedipus or *The Bacchae*, or Rome's founding on the murder of Remus by his brother Romulus, or countless others from the six habitated continents. All result from a sacrificial crisis which is solved by the killing of one individual.

In the Bible, Cain slays his brother Abel, the first murder mentioned, and goes on to found Cainite culture. It is important to note that Cainite culture predates Jewish culture, and is thus not Jewish culture as such. The murder is truly foundational. However, unlike all other similar myths around the world, where those killed are viewed as guilty or at least the killings are presented as justifiable, the Bible proclaims, for the first time, *the innocence of the victim*. This view is repeated not only in Genesis and Exodus (where Moses and the entire Jewish people are the victims) but in the later books, such as Job, Jeremiah, Hosea and the second Isaiah. One of Judaism's members, during the reign of the first two Roman emperors, would study these texts and gain a greater anthropological understanding of the origin of man than anyone before or since.

−December 2013

Chapter Thirty-three

The Abyss

Henry Adams, our greatest 19th century historian, lived across the street from the White House where his grandfather John Quincy had once resided. At a dinner party during World War I, an assistant secretary of the Navy was extolling the virtues of then-President Woodrow Wilson. "Young man," exclaimed Adams, pointing out the window, "it doesn't make the slightest difference who lives in that house. History goes on with or without the president." And so was admonished assistant secretary Franklin Delano Roosevelt.

FDR notwithstanding, history has generally proven Adams right. Take the 2012 election. Please. Its vapid uselessness, useless because this year's major two party candidates have not addressed the issues of vital importance to the nation and world, is currently on full display on the U.S. East Coast. Political operatives-charlatans who have raised and spent hundreds of millions of dollars with the singular purpose of dulling the eyes and ears of the American electorate-may now pause and regroup as the latest of this year's climate change-induced events immobilizes a quarter of the country.

Global warming is real. The fact that the criminally negligent corporate media (by that I mean *all* of it) has refused until now to mention the terrifying fact of our era in the same breath as "once in a lifetime" weather related events that now occur as frequently as Hallmark holidays, gives hope, one would think, to starving lawyers in need of pursuing defendants with deep pockets. Bought and paid for by the fossil fuel industry, these elite purveyors of information, to keep the public somnolent, provided one-tenth as many climate change stories in 2011 as in 2007, despite the mounting verifying information of the phenomena.

Sandy, the most aptly named hurricane ever, has wreaked havoc, fueled by a five degree warmer than normal ocean temperature, with but a taste of what's to come. Sandy is short for Cassandra, the Trojan prophetess in Greek mythology who could foretell the future, though no one believed her. Our modern Cassandras are the world's scientists who have been warning of this warming for more than two decades; our myopic leaders have chosen to ignore them.

Barack Obama first gave us a taste of his moral stature in his silent acquiescence of the Israeli massacre of over 1400 Palestinians in late 2008-early 2009. It was confirmed by his lunatic capitulation to MICMAC (the Military Industrial Congressional Media Academic Complex) in escalating the Afghanistan debacle, costing thousands of more lives and wasting billions of more dollars. His trifecta was achieved by December 2009, when at the Copenhagen Summit for climate change mitigation, perhaps our last real chance of tackling the issue, he conspired with the leader of fellow giant carbon emitter China to do nothing.

It should be noted, in fairness, that Mitt Romney was fully supportive of Obama in all three areas, and now of the drones which have killed thousands of Muslims at the push of a land-borne U.S. pilot button. Polls taken inside Mitt's head are inconclusive as to whether he genuinely believes in Obama's barbarism, or merely is kowtowing to the most ignorant members of his party (in other words, his base), in order to have a chance at fulfilling his dream of becoming official spokesman for Multinational Corporations United. David Bromwich notes that "the party he (Romney) represents has ceased to be a collective rational agent for working on the problems of the modern world."

In three "debates," no mention of Obama's shredding of the Constitution, expanding the U.S. Empire to the precipice of bankruptcy, or climate change, was ever made. This was by design.

The Commission on Presidential Debates, formed in 1987 by the Democratic and Republican parties to maintain control over the questions and exclude third parties, runs these charades. The League of Women Voters immediately withdrew, after being given a list of demands by the two parties because giving in to it, in the League's words, "would perpetrate a fraud on the American voter."

The fraud has blossomed nicely for the two parties. The Commission, wholly corporate owned, has seven sponsors, led by Anheuser- Busch, so This Bud's for You prudently covers both the World Series and Presidential Showdowns. It insists that for a third candidate to qualify he or she must have 15% of popular support in five national polls, while of course the Elite Media makes sure, by virtually never mentioning alternative candidates, that this cannot occur. It's the perfect Catch-22.

Bromwich and 12 other liberal stalwarts, including the venerable Garry Wills, gave their views on the election in the current *New York Review* of *Books*. None, seeing Obama's lack of accomplishments in four years, could give an actual reason why the incumbent should be retained, other than that the challenger would be worse. Probably so. But some choice voters are left with in our now completely dysfunctional political system. How long history will go on, Henry Adams didn't say.

−November 2012

The Answer

"I will utter what has been hidden since the foundation of the world"

-Matthew 13:35

Less than one year into Barack Obama's second term, MICMAC media blares about continual information regarding 2016 presidential aspirants. This insults all viewers, of course, except those inside the rigged game itself-the political consultants, hucksters, and advertisers who perpetuate the now never-pausing election cycle and the next-to-nonexistent governing process. The answer to solving any of the nation's or world's gigantic problems does not appear likely to hail from the modern two-party political system, as vicious a non-violent example of mimetic rivalry as can be observed. This rivalry now threatens to spiral out of control, with both sides more resembling each other as they howl at one another following MICMAC media's made-up controversies grabbing their limited attention spans, which involve mainly the raising of money for the next election.

Two millennia ago the itinerant preacher Jesus of Nazareth studied the Scriptures which today's Christians call the Old Testament, including the words "For I desire mercy and not sacrifice, and acknowledgement of God rather than burnt offerings" (Hosea 6:6). Exposing the world's lie about its own cultural origins, he succinctly told those around him, "You belong to your father the devil, and you want to carry out the desires of your father. He was a murderer from the beginning, and does not stand in the truth, because there is no truth in him" (John 8:44).

Jesus then invited the enmity of all who participated in the sacrificial system of his milieu-the Romans, the Jews (Pharisees and Sadducees), and the mob-an earlier triumvirate of the power structure which today is replicated in America by MICMAC, the supporting 9%, and the bottom 90%. All of us are guilty to the extent we wish the sacrificial system to succeed as in times of old. If today our scapegoats are Muslims, in the guise of "Islamic terrorism," it is patently revealed these scapegoats are, once again, innocent, for it is preposterous to condemn 1.5 billion persons for the actions of at most a few thousand, who in many cases are being reactive to the oppressive power structures MICMAC sustains.

Jesus, in fact, tells all that the sacrificial system is no longer relevant, that "Love your foes" is a *structural* (and not merely utopian) basis for living, and that by doing the opposite we only perpetuate the unending cycle of violence. He has been, through the Gospels, telling us this for two thousand years, but men are slow learners, and the vestiges of the sacrificial system die hard. The Roman Catholic Church itself maintains, mainly through the obscure, anonymous, and late addition to the New Testament canon Letter to the Hebrews, that the death of Christ on the cross was sacrificial, as if it had been wanted by God the Father as ransom for mankind's sins.

Rene Girard, the world's foremost anthropological philosopher, radically asserts that the death of Christ can be easily interpreted as non-sacrificial (*Things Hidden Since the Foundation of the World*, pp. 180-223) via the Gospels.* Garry Wills says Christ's only sacrifice is the "offering of his innocent body to the fury of the sacrificial system" itself, and that the Holy Spirit "breathes through all religious life, in every Christian denomination," and "among Jews, Buddhists, Muslims and others."

The innocence of victims has thus been revealed once and for all, but that does not mean victims do not continue to be slaughtered. Unfortunately they are still being killed, only they no longer provide temporary pacification for cultures that previously sacrificed ones like them. The shackles of the old sacrificial system have been unlocked, and *all against all* violence once again threatens, only now on a planetary scale. Therefore, it will take leadership aware of the victimary mechanism to publicize the world's foundational lie, and preach a message based on truth. At present, none on the U.S. national scene have demonstrated they are aware of the mechanism, at least in the field of politics.

In March 2013, though, few could have predicted that a man about to enter onto the world stage had a profound awareness of Truth, an indomitable empathy for the poor and suffering, and the apparent saintliness to imitate Christ in a manner that invites all to follow. Jorge Mario Bergoglio, elected Pope after the first voluntary pontifical resignation in over seven centuries, chose the name Francis in honor of one of the most deservedly revered figures in history, St. Francis of Assisi. He has bluntly and forcefully attacked the world's unregulated capitalist system as "tyranny," and, with the help of the Holy Spirit, may help do to this tyranny what Pope John Paul II assisted in doing for the tyranny of communism.

Naïve people who tend to sympathize with either of these tyrannies reflexively label opponents of their sympathies followers of the other camp, but the late Chalmers Johnson may have said it best when summing up a perspective of the West in the late U.S./ Soviet square-off, "We didn't win the Cold War. Both sides lost. They just lost it first." With at least 90% of the U.S. population economically worse off two decades after the collapse of the Red Menace, the Cold War is indeed proving to be the most Pyrrhic victory since the Greeks "defeated" the Romans in the 270s BCE.

What is needed now, argues Girard collaborator Jean-Michel Oughourlian, is that Clausewitz (the supreme observer of war) be "healed" with Machiavelli (the political strategist without peer). But to reduce the escalation to extremes with a moderating politics would require "politicians be sages, ready to acknowledge the mimetic otherness of their own desires." Can it be that there are at least a few of them, soon to be in high enough office, waiting for the opportunity to serve their electorates before it is too late? *That is the question of the hour.*

—December 15, 2013

---

* Girard later rejected this non-sacrificial reading (*The One by Whom Scandal Comes*, p.40-45), but the role of Jesus as scapegoat supreme remains central to his theory of revealing the origin of man's violence, and Christ being "the perfect sacrifice that puts an end to all the others."

Acknowledgements

Tom "Top Cat" Costello (once again) and Jason "JP3" Price of Word Association; Antiwar.com for being a refreshing antidote to MICMAC media; Jeffrey D. Pepper, whose Common Dreams include more Michigan State Spartan titles; the Elite Eleven (see p.133); Angela Marino, a Noble replacement; my trio of high achieving *Falconiformes*; and lastly, The Candidate–"without question, the best of the Plaweckis,"–and that's from a higher and more neutral authority than the author.

WA